Happy Living for New Homemakers

By The Editors of
MODERN BRIDE Magazine
and Evelyn Enright

Ziff-Davis Publishing Company
American Bride Publications Division
New York, New York

$8.95

ii

Acknowledgments

Putting this book together took a great deal of cooperative effort and those responsible did so with dedication to the project. Our special thanks to Evelyn Enright, Terry Dufka of Carson Pirie Scott, and staff members, Carolyn Bartel, Home Furnishings Editor and Gail Scott, Copy Editor.

Cele Goldsmith Lalli
Editor
MODERN BRIDE Magazine

Book cover: "Fair Ellen," courtesy of Raintree Designs by Laura Ashley

Photography credits: pages 33, 34, 35, 55, 65, 69, 70, 71, 89, Lisanti; page 36, Simon Scott Brown; page 72 Fritz Taggart; pages 107, 108, 142, 143, Bill Margerin; pages 105, 106, Jerry Friedman; page 141, Bernard Vidal; page 144, Harry Hartman.

Contents

Introduction

To help you plan your wedding and set up your home for a new life together, the Editors of MODERN BRIDE Magazine draw on the editorial experience of many years for the detailed information you will find in this book.

We realize the significance of a beautiful wedding and the importance of beginning a new life as a partner, wife, mother, and homemaker. If, in addition, you are also a working wife, you will have even more responsibilities and less time to execute them.

An attractive and smoothly run home is a decided plus in your new married life, and you'll appreciate the refuge and security a home can give you and the pride and pleasure you will feel when the home is furnished and decorated to your taste.

With a little experience and the help of the good advice in these pages, your own home can be exactly what you want it to be . . . a happy place where you can enjoy each other in privacy or in the company of good friends.

The charm and beauty of your home does not depend on the amount of money you spend, but more on the care and taste you use in choosing the furnishings. We do not suggest that you necessarily complete the entire decorating scheme at once, but rather have a long-range plan that can be brought together as the time and funds become available.

We hope that within these covers you will find the guidance you need for planning a perfect wedding and a home that is exactly right for both of you now and in the years to come.

The Editors,
MODERN BRIDE Magazine

Chapter 1
Planning Your Wedding

Your wedding is the most important event in your life. Not only does it unite you and your fiancé, but it brings your two families together. Whether you want a small intimate wedding or a large formal one, it requires careful planning and attention to details to assure a smooth running, wonderfully memorable day.

Because there are so many elements to put together, it is never too early to begin making arrangements once you've settled on a date. Popular reception sites are in great demand and are often booked a year or more in advance. All wedding gowns and bridesmaids' dresses are custom ordered and take at least two months to be delivered for the first fitting. To avoid confusion and disappointment, you must allow as much time as possible.

This chapter is organized to give you a thorough planning guide from the time you announce your engagement to the moment you become husband and wife. If you follow this calendar of priorities, adapting it as you go along to your family traditions and your personal preferences, you will be relaxed and ready to enjoy every second of your wedding day.

Announcing Your Engagement

Announcements should be sent to the newspapers, both in your home town and your fiancé's, if he lives elsewhere. Type or print all information. Indicate the date when you would like the announcement to appear. Allow plenty of time; if in doubt, check with the society editor as to when copy should be in her hands. Be sure your name, address, and telephone number are on the upper right-hand corner of the page.

Many papers and some photographers have forms on which to fill in your name, your fiancé's name, names and residences of both sets of parents, background material on you both, and the expected date of your wedding. Society editors determine how much of this they can use. You may send a photograph to the newspapers with your announcement, if you wish. An eight-by-ten-inch glossy is preferable, with caption attached— written on a separate piece of paper, not on the back. Even if not used, this photograph will not be returned.

An Engagement Party

Often the bride's family wishes to celebrate the official announcement with a party for the couple. If the bride's family lives a great distance away, the groom's parents may do this, if they wish. It is *absolutely essential* that both the bride and her fiancé be at the engagement party. If for any reason this is not possible (military separation, school separation, etc.), the party must wait until they are both able to attend.

The engagement party usually includes relatives and close friends and is given in the form of a cocktail party, dinner, or even a summer barbecue. Informal printed invitations should read: first line—your parents' name (or his, if they are hosts); second line— your name (or his); third line—"To meet Thomas Johnson (or Jane Jones)." Handwritten or telephone invitations are also correct.

The Bride's Calendar

FOUR TO TWELVE MONTHS BEFORE THE WEDDING

Decide what kind of wedding. Your gown, men's attire, and number of attendants determine formality. Budget is also an important consideration in deciding how large and how formal the wedding should be.

Choose time of day. Religion, climate, local custom, and the place you wish to hold the reception all influence the time.

Set the wedding date. Reserve the place where you will have the reception. Call on your clergyman with your fiancé.

Decide on number of attendants. Invite the friends you choose. Even in the smallest wedding you will each have one attendant.

Draw up the guest list. Usually the bride's family bears the financial responsibility for both wedding and reception. If so, and budgetary limitations require that the reception list be limited, the groom's family traditionally is allowed fewer guests.

Enroll with a bridal consultant. The consultant in your favorite store can give you expert advice, and her services are free.

Choose your gown. Aware of current styles from reading your bridal magazine, you probably have an idea of what you want and can choose from designs in all price ranges.

Choose bridesmaids' dresses. Rely on your bridal consultant to help coordinate color and style in your wedding party.

Plan future home furnishings. Choose china, silver, crystal patterns and register, these selections in the Bridal Gift Registry. Obtain a floor plan of your apartment or house and, with your fiancé, begin to look for basic furniture and accessories.

THREE MONTHS BEFORE THE WEDDING

Plan the reception. The most important clue to its success is a good caterer. Old established firms are usually the best and must be reserved well in advance, but it's worth it. In the long run, they are less expensive because you get what you pay for. However, even with the best, get detailed estimates including menu, decorations, and liquor. Never sign a contract without checking it out thoroughly. A good banquet manager or caterer can be a tremendous help, so ask questions and rely on his experience.

Plan your music. Confirm time and day of wedding and rehearsal with organist, soloist, choir, and musicians for the reception. Go over selections carefully and consult with your fiancé for preferences. When selecting the group to play at your reception, be sure to buy continuous music, even at additional cost.

See your florist. Remember your budget and know something of what you want before you talk to him. Your bridal consultant can help with ideas for the church decorations and the banquet manager or caterer will have some guidelines for floral designs at hotel, club, or home reception. Of course, an experienced florist will be your best source of advice.

Select a photographer. Once again, go to the most reputable—a professional who specializes in wedding work. Look at examples of his work and ask questions! If you plan to have a formal bridal portrait taken before the wedding, arrange for your sitting just as soon as the gown is ready. Should you prefer one photographer's portrait and another photographer's candids, you can engage them separately. Costs vary with location, number of poses and prints, and black and white or color photographs. Get an estimate of the costs from the photographer before hiring him. Whoever you choose, remember that your wedding album becomes a family treasure that always carries you back to that wonderful moment.

Order your invitations. Traditional formal invitations are usually engraved. However, a form of printing that resembles engraving and is considerably less expensive is sometimes used and is currently acceptable. For more informal weddings, pastel-tinted invitations with engraving or printing in matched ink is also recently popular. Order from your jeweler, stationer, or department store. All have qualified consultants to guide you in choice of paper, style of lettering, and correct wording, no matter how complicated. Allow ample time for delivery. If you wish, you can obtain the plain outer and inner envelopes early and address them ahead.

Order wedding announcements. These may be sent to friends who have not been invited to the wedding and should be mailed so that they will be received a day or two after the wedding takes place. You can get advice on style when ordering invitations.

Order personal stationery. You will be writing many thank-you notes both before and after your wedding, so order an ample supply of letter and note paper at the same time. White, ivory, or pale pastel informal notes, either plain or with your initial engraved in simple letters, are always in good taste.

Plan your wedding trip. Your fiancé is responsible for making all arrangements for the honeymoon destination—getting tickets, reservations, etc. This is easily done through a travel agent who can give you expert advice with no charge for the service.

Begin shopping for your trousseau. Remember that you will be wearing your trousseau during the first year of your married life, so choose clothes in relation to where and how you are going to live. Select your going-away outfit and honeymoon clothes after you have agreed upon plans for your honeymoon destination.

Mothers choose their gowns. Your mother has the privilege of choosing first so that she may have the color and style she prefers. The groom's mother picks a gown of the same length and color to complement. Both should blend with the bridal party colors.

Visit your doctor. Make an appointment for the required tests and a complete medical checkup. If a premarital test for rubella is not included among the required tests, this is an ideal time to request that your doctor administer it.

TWO MONTHS BEFORE THE WEDDING

Plan recording of gifts. From the moment the first gift arrives, it is wise to keep accurate records either in a special book (there are many designed for this purpose) or in your invitation card files.

Displaying your gifts. These may be shown at your home, in a room set aside for this, for a week before the wedding. Gifts of a similar nature should be grouped together. Be sure that you have adequate insurance against loss or damage to your gifts.

Keep up with thank-you notes. Try to acknowledge each gift upon arrival, to avoid last-minute rush and lengthy delays in extending thanks.

Finish addressing invitations. All addressing, stuffing, stamping should be done as early as possible so that you will be free to write thank-you notes, tend to last-minute details, and enjoy attending parties that are being given especially in your honor.

Plan rehearsal dinner. Select a time and place, settle upon menu and decorative details with the caterer. Notify your attendants and the groom's family when and where it will be held.

Plan accommodations for guests. If you cannot put up your attendants or arrange for them to stay with friends or neighbors, make hotel reservations for them. Your fiancé does the same.

Select gifts for attendants. Usually the bride gives something personal and permanent to her attendants—a charm, pin, bracelet, etc. Often the gifts are alike, but the maid of honor may receive something special. Remind your fiancé to select presents for his best man and ushers. Cuff links, tie bar, money clip, small leather goods are some suggestions.

Marriage license. Check with local authorities on waiting periods for blood tests and obtain a license. Go with fiancé to get the license.

ONE MONTH BEFORE THE WEDDING

Select wedding ring. Often this is done earlier when you are choosing your engagement ring. If not, you and your fiancé should settle upon one now and be sure to allow time for engraving.

Have hair styled. Make an appointment with your hairstylist to have your hair done as you want it to look on your wedding day.

Attend parties in your honor. Showers for the bride are held during this time. These may be given by members of the wedding party, friends, co-workers, cousins, or aunts, but not by members of your immediate family or of your fiancé's. There are many kinds of showers that are fun and practical and do not require lavish gifts: kitchen, linen, wine, flowers and plants, to name only a few. Discussing the guest list with the bride is a wise move. In this way, the hostess can keep the party small enough to be intimate, as traditionally intended, and the bride can split the invitations enough to prevent her friends from attending so many showers that the purchase of gifts becomes overburdening. Thank-you notes to those in attendance are not necessary, but do acknowledge those sent in absentia.

Final fitting on your gown. Avoid last-minute panic by having the final fitting on your gown no less than four weeks before the date. Bring actual shoes and undergarments for your gown.

Have formal portrait taken. Often you can arrange to have your formal wedding portrait taken when you have your final fitting. Otherwise, it is taken at the photographer's studio just as soon as the gown is ready. Order glossy prints, if you intend to send photographs to the newspapers with the announcements.

Mail invitations. They should be received three weeks before the wedding.

Check apparel for wedding party. Have bridesmaids' gowns fitted. Shoe heel height should be the same at fitting as on day of wedding. Get swatches of material and have shoes dyed to match. If any attendants live out-of-town, send their dresses so they can be fitted properly. Check mothers' dresses and accessories.

Plan transportation for the wedding party. Arrange for limousines or some other form of transportation to take the wedding party to church and reception.

Check with caterer. Order wedding cake and make final decision on the reception menu. Give caterer a reliable estimate on the number of guests so he can give you a written confirmation of cost per person—with an itemized accounting.

Confer with photographer. Be sure he/she knows what candids you wish to have taken so that people who are special to you will be included in your album.

Keep gift checklist up-to-date. Many of the things you need will be received as shower or wedding gifts and checked off as they arrive. Note the essentials that are missing so you can make special requests if asked what you still would like to have.

Plan the bridesmaids' luncheon. If you are not having very many attendants and can arrange to have this at home, it will lend a more personal touch. Present gifts now or at the rehearsal dinner.

Find place for the bridesmaids to dress. Make arrangements for bridesmaids to dress where they can all be together, whether in your home, at a friend's house, in a hotel room, or in the church.

Know details of the ceremony. Go over all procedures of the ceremony and receiving line with your fiancé and all the attendants.

Select groom's wedding gift. Often the bride wishes to give her groom a gift, especially if it is not a double-ring ceremony.

Plan seating arrangements. Arrange seating plans for the rehearsal dinner (if it is large) and for the reception. Write out place cards, if you are having a bride's table and a parents' table.

Arrange for moving. If you will be living in another town, arrange to have gifts and your personal belongings shipped. Usually this is not done until after the wedding, especially if gifts are displayed. Consult movers in advance for estimates and make sure you are insured against damage or loss in transit.

TWO WEEKS BEFORE THE WEDDING

Thank-you notes. No matter how busy you are, do not get behind in acknowledging your gifts.

Final check. Be sure clothing and accessories for all members of the bridal party are in order. Settle on final details with caterer.

Announcements. Send write-up and photos to papers in your town and in the groom's hometown.

Traffic plans. Arrange with the police department for an officer to handle traffic and parking at ceremony and reception.

Name changes. See to name changes on your bank account, social security records, license, charge accounts, etc.

Trousseau. Make sure your honeymoon trousseau is complete and begin to pack for the trip.

ONE WEEK BEFORE THE WEDDING

Final consultations. Have one more meeting with the people responsible for seeing that your wedding and the reception go smoothly. Give caterer the final figure on guests.

Special aide. Appoint a friend (not a member of your immediate family who is apt to have too much on his or her mind to be effective) to handle last-minute phone calls, wires, and anything else that comes up.

Wedding rehearsal. This takes place the day or evening before the wedding and everyone who is to participate in the wedding ceremony should be present. Line up bridesmaids and ushers according to height, determine the speed of the procession with the organist or other musician(s), and go through everything but the words. The rehearsal dinner takes place afterward.

What to Wear?

Formal wedding. BRIDE: white, ivory, or pastel-tinted dress, with any length train. Long veil covering the train, or making the train; if shorter than fingertip, then very full with many layers. BRIDESMAIDS: long dress matching or harmonizing with other maids' dresses in style, color; simple cap or hat. HONOR ATTENDANT: long dress coordinated with maids' in color and style. MOTHERS: long dresses in harmonizing color. MEN: traditional cutaway coat, striped trousers, gray waistcoat, white pleated-bosom shirt. Or, more contemporary contoured long or short jacket, striped trousers, wing-collared shirt, gray vest. Same style jacket in selection of colors, matching pants, and coordinated shirt. After 6:00 P.M., white tie, black tails.

Semiformal wedding. BRIDE: dress in white, ivory, or delicate tints, floor-length or with chapel train. Short or long veil—if short, very full. BRIDESMAIDS and MOTHERS: same as formal. MEN: Oxford gray stroller, gray striped trousers, gray waistcoat, white pleated-bosom shirt, turn-down collar. Or, formal suit in a choice of colors and contemporary styling; matching or contrasting trousers, white or colored shirt. Bow tie, vest, or cummerbund.

Informal. BRIDE: long or short dress, in white or pastel tones or an afternoon dress or suit. Short veil or bridal-type hat. BRIDES-MAIDS: same length as bride or, if bride wears long dress, short dress is permissible. MOTHERS: street-length dress. MEN: dark gray or navy business suit. In summer, white or natural-color jacket, dark trousers; or navy jacket, white trousers.

Who Pays for What?

The Bride: wedding ring for groom, if it's a double-ring ceremony; wedding gift for groom; presents and accommodations for her attendants; personal stationery; medical examination.

The Groom: marriage license; his medical examination; engagement and wedding rings for the bride; bride's bouquet and going-away corsage (bride's family may pay for this if they wish to); boutonnieres for the men and corsages for both mothers; gloves, ascots or ties for the men in the wedding party; wedding gift for bride; gifts for the best man and ushers; fee for the clergyman; the honeymoon; the bachelor dinner (optional).

The Bride's Family: bride's personal trousseau (wedding gown, headpiece, veil, etc., going-away outfit); wedding invitations, enclosure cards for the reception; announcements; formal engagement and wedding photographs and candids; soloist, sexton (if not included in price of church); aisle carpet, canopy; flowers; gratuity for traffic policemen if it's a large wedding; transportation for bridal party; bridesmaids' luncheon; rehearsal dinner (the groom's family may wish to pay for this); the entire cost of the reception.

The Groom's Family: clothes they wear to the wedding; traveling expenses and hotel bills; wedding gift for the couple; the wedding rehearsal dinner (optional).

The Attendants: their wedding clothes and accessories; their own traveling expenses; wedding gifts to the bride and groom.

The Guests: any traveling expenses and hotel bills; wedding gifts to the couple.

How to Use the Bridal Gift Registry

Decide with your fiancé what style you want in china, crystal, and silver. Also come to an agreement on linens. Together figure out the kitchenware you will need. Take these preferences to the gift consultant in a hometown department store.

On your first visit she will give you a complete checklist on which to fill in all of the items you desire. She will go over each selection with you, answer questions, and clear up any confusions you may have. If you are having difficulty compromising on patterns, etc., ask the consultant to show you what is available throughout the store.

As you go around the store, add other items that you see you will need or want to the checklist. The consultant will use this to direct friends and relatives in their choice of gifts for you. It is up to you to inform people that you have registered at a particular store. Make an effort to select gifts in a variety of price ranges so all friends can take advantage of this service.

If your fiancé lives in a different city, you can split your registry preferences and give some to a store in his hometown. Have your fiancé's mother tell their friends the store you have chosen. You can also use two or three prominent stores in your own town. Be sure to tell out-of-towners the names of the stores in which you are registered. If you receive gifts from other sources, it is your obligation to phone the registries and have the items removed from the checklist. This will minimize the need to return gifts later.

What do you really need to live the way you want? How do you go about making the right decisions and then acquiring the basic home furnishings items necessary to create a home for two?

These questions are undoubtedly turning over in your mind as you plan right now for your wedding, and your wonderful new life.

How to Determine What You Need

The home you are about to create will be a very special and personal kind of environment for the two of you. There are many things you are going to need right now, others you will want to acquire in the near future, and still others that your parents or friends may consider essential to their life-style, but you feel are unnecessary. At the outset, it's vital to determine who you are and what is important to both of you. Answering these questions should prove helpful in getting you started.

What kind of living space will you have? Even if you haven't yet signed the lease, you have some idea of what you can afford in the area where you plan to live. If it's a studio with kitchen, you'll be thinking in terms of more dual-purpose furniture, including a sleep sofa of some kind, while if you are lucky enough to have a separate bedroom, there is a choice of bed sizes to be made and a lot more furniture items will be on your list.

How long can you reasonably expect to be there? None of us has a crystal ball, but plans for the future do have a way of materializing. Generally, newly married young couples are upwardly mobile, already on their way to bigger and better housing. That's why it makes good sense to plan ahead, putting the bulk of your money into possessions you can take with you. Good quality bedding, linens, tablewares, and versatile, basic furniture are sensible investments. On the other hand, it's wise to avoid or spend as little as possible on window treatments that may not fit a new dwelling, built-ins that cannot be dismantled easily and refit elsewhere, or installed carpeting that may have to be left behind.

How do you both like to live? What you decide to buy will be determined largely by the kind of life-style you have dreams of establishing. If you thrive on entertaining, you will want to plan on extra seating in the living room, a dining table that expands, extra kitchen and serving equipment for guests. You may want to furnish and arrange your home to accommodate arts, crafts or hobby activities, or set aside special areas of the living room or bedroom for reading, studying, listening to music, and other quiet pastimes. The priorities on your shopping list will depend on your own particular interests. You'll find this subject elaborated upon in the chapter entitled "Making Floor Plans for Each Room."

What can you afford to include in the budget right now? Since few couples have all the money they need to buy everything all at once, furnishing a first home comes down to a matter of making choices. It is well to keep in mind, as you plan and shop, that the purchase of some items might have to be delayed in favor of getting the best possible quality in what is essential right now. Elsewhere in this book, you'll find decorating ideas for filling in the bare spots temporarily.

Seeking Help When Needed

During the months ahead, you are going to make a lot of decisions, many of which involve items you'll have around, hopefully, for a long time. While the whole idea is exciting and adventuresome, it is wise to think before you buy and, wherever possible, to take advantage of the expert sources of help available to you.

First and foremost, your own knowledge about yourselves. Your own past can be helpful as an indicator of what you need and what you can very well do without for now. One or both of you has undoubtedly set up housekeeping before, whether on a college campus or the apartment in town that went with your first job. While these quarters had an air of transience, you did learn something about what you expect from life at home.

Perhaps you never really liked the color scheme or furniture style and now yearn for something else. If you rushed out to buy furniture without first making a floor plan, you may have found it didn't fit in as well as you expected or that some purchases weren't all that useful. You may have spent too much money on some items and had no budget left over for good lamps, end tables, linens, and other essentials of comfortable living. Think about all the things that were right and wrong about previous dwellings, and reap the benefit of your experiences now. Learn also from the mistakes and triumphs of people you know. Analyze the homes you visit and ask yourselves which features you would choose or reject.

Department and specialty store bridal gift registry consultants, as detailed in Chapter 1. A trained expert in helping engaged couples select what they need, a gift registry consultant can be an important person in your life right now. This service is undoubtedly the best and most efficient method for making sure gifts a bride receives are what she really wants and needs. While it's important to register your preferences early, do wait until you have done all the necessary shopping, soul-searching, and planning.

Interior designers. Department and furniture stores often have a design staff available to help in a number of different ways. If you simply want advice on a particular problem, such questions may be answered free of charge as a customer service. If you decide to have a decorator supervise the complete planning of your home, the service is usually free if you agree to buy a certain amount of merchandise. There are also many interior design firms where, if you don't want the whole treatment, you can pay a fee and have someone work out floor plans and color schemes for you to follow through on your own.

Magazines, books and model room displays. There's a lot to be learned about yourselves just by browsing through stores or home furnishings shows and looking at books and magazines, particularly those directed to brides and grooms, apartment dwellers, and newly married couples. Together, you can discuss each display or photograph and find out very quickly not only which styles, color, and moods have the most appeal, but which furnishings should be on your list in order to provide for your needs.

The bride's checklist. A wonderfully simple but efficient way of making sure you haven't overlooked anything is the Bride's Checklist, which you'll find in the last chapter of this book. This very thorough listing covers all the essential home furnishings items by category so you can check off what you need and keep a record of items purchased or received as gifts.

Thinking Your Project Through

In essence, the best way to go about furnishing a home is to put off making any purchases until you have gone through every stage of planning and have a clear idea in mind of what the finished product will contain and how well it will function. If you buy something right the first time, you won't have to buy that item again until it wears out. This is the real measure of a shrewd shopper.

The chapters that follow are intended to supply the guidelines you need along every step of the way. Follow them as you would a recipe you haven't tried before, reading through to the end to find out what ingredients and preparations are required, then going back to the beginning and proceeding one step at a time.

Chapter 3
Deciding Which Furniture Styles Appeal to You

oday, we no longer think of furnishing a home as committing ourselves to a specific style or definite period in design. Rather, a home is the expression of the personal tastes and attitude toward life of two individuals who have many and varied interests.

Your design preferences are a result of your backgrounds and experiences, including family environment, education, travel, and cultural interests. As time goes on and you share more experiences together, your taste will probably change. If the furniture and accessories chosen for your first home are of good basic design and quality, most of them will adapt to your future needs, perhaps with a change of fabric or finish to blend in with an entirely new decorating theme.

Perhaps both of you are sold on one particular style or period right now, but it's still nice to know that eclectic decorating—or the bringing together of all the things you like, regardless of their place in time or national origin—is a trend that seems here to stay. A very personal kind of style that makes a lot of sense, eclectic decorating is no more than the melting pot theory applied to interior design. It's the simplicity of an American-designed Parsons table providing contrast for an English traditional or Colonial sofa. It's the Oriental rug you were lucky enough to inherit looking better than ever under a modern steel and glass cocktail table that allows the pattern and colors to show through.

How to Determine What's Right for You

The kinds of furniture you'll be considering may be classified in three distinct categories—traditional, provincial, and contemporary (also referred to as modern). Each is described and illustrated in the last part of this chapter.

To decide which style or combination of styles is right for you, here are some preliminary steps worth taking:

Spend an evening together looking through home furnishings magazines, books, and catalogs. Discuss what you like and don't like, until a pattern emerges. Keep notes and clippings.

Take lots of field trips. Model room settings in department or home furnishings stores, home furnishings and antique shows, and museums with furniture galleries are invaluable aids. So are restoration villages and the restored homes of famous persons. Be alert to everything around you—even the decor of a favorite restaurant or ski lodge may yield clues to your design preferences.

Think about formality and informality. If yours is a strictly casual way of life, you'll feel more at home with the easy lines of modern design or the cozy, nostalgic air conveyed by provincial. If

you enjoy dressing up for formal dinners and dances, the luxuriousness of Eighteenth-Century English or other popular traditional styles will undoubtedly give you great pleasure. Remember,
too, that casual furniture styles call for equally casual fabrics, like
sailcloth, cotton, and nubby tweeds. More formal furniture, traditionally, teams best with brocades, satins, velvets, and other rich
textures. If denims are the mainstay of your wardrobe, chances are
you'll go for furniture in a similar mood.

Consider what you now have, for better or for worse. If either or
both of you already have usable furniture, give some thought to
how well you like it or which pieces you like better than others.
You may have the nucleus for furnishing your home in similar style
—or you may have your heart set on something else. While it's a
great boost to the budget to start off with some furniture, don't buy
new pieces to harmonize with a style you are not really crazy about
just to save money. Different syles make an interesting mix in the
same room—but it's the idea that you like each individual piece
that makes the whole thing work for you personally.

How to Recognize Good Basic Design

Just what is good, basic furniture design that fits in anywhere? You
might compare it to the well-tailored suit or well-cut dress that
always seems right for any occasion.

The more furniture you look at, particularly in room settings or
photographs of interiors, the more easily you will recognize
designs that adapt well to a variety of situations. Following are
some examples of good, all-around pieces:

Lawson or Tuxedo sofas, particularly in lengths of six or seven
feet, have simple lines, so, depending on your choice of fabric,

you have a fitting companion for furniture of almost every design persuasion. Also adaptable are sectionals or modular grouping that can be used individually or together to form seating areas. Less versatile are designs with more complex lines and curves, like Victorian, Duncan Phyfe, and some of the more formal French designs. Upholstered furniture chosen to fit a specific wall area, as a curved and sectional, may not be as useful should you move to another apartment.

Club, Lawson, arm, or other simple styles in chairs. If the chair can be fitted with a well-tailored slipcover or is mostly wood with a slip-seat or separate seat cushion, changes can be made easily and inexpensively when necessary.

Modular storage pieces in contemporary or modified traditional styles. Bachelor chests or cabinets that can be placed side by side or used separately according to how much unbroken wall space is available are more versatile than items like triple dressers. Look, too, for storage furniture that does not have a distinct bedroom, dining, or living room look for additional versatility.

Bookshelves or bookcases you can add on to. While an entire wall system of shelves, drawers, and cabinets is expensive to acquire all at once, you can buy a few sections at a time and eventually complete the unit. Wall units make efficient use of space and also provide a place to show off the personal treasures that do so much to individualize a room.

Once you've acquired enough basics—perhaps a sofa, two chairs, tables, and some storage for the living room; a bed and enough drawer space for the bedroom—you may want to round out your collection with a few accent pieces that are not only functional, but fun. An unusual wicker or rattan chair is a nice contrast for wood furniture in the bedroom, while an interesting old curio cabinet, desk, or period chair can bring distinction to a living

room. Think in terms of varying shapes, too. If all your furniture is square or rectangular, add a round table, barrel chair, or other curved piece for greater geometric interest.

Guide to Period Furniture

For centuries, furniture design has been a direct result of important economic and historical events. When the great reigning monarchs of Europe were frivolous and fun-loving, furniture became ornate and feminine, while more serious-minded kings were apt to influence revivals of the classic lines of Rome and Greece. These economic facts of life are clearly stated in the early furniture of the American colonies—at first crude and simple, gradually taking on elegance and grace as the settlers prospered. The growth of transportation has been another catalyst. By the twentieth century, rapid travel and good communications made it possible for designers from all over the world to inspire each other as they sought to break completely from the past and perfect the style we now call modern or contemporary—a truly international concept that gradually evolved out of Germany, France, Scandinavia, America, the Oriental nations, etc. Today, the furniture available fits into three major classifications—traditional, provincial, contemporary or modern. Here are descriptions of each.

Traditional

Traditional furniture may be compared to the classics in literature, music, painting, or any other art form. Just as a Shakespearean play or a Rembrandt painting is still enjoyable today, so has the

Guide to Period Furniture

QUEEN ANNE
(EARLY 18TH CENTURY)

CHIPPENDALE
(MIDDLE 18TH CENTURY)

ADAM
(LATE 18TH CENTURY)

HEPPLEWHITE
(LATE 18TH AND
EARLY 19TH CENTURIES)

SHERATON
(LATE 18TH AND
EARLY 19TH CENTURIES)

LOUIS XIV
(LATE 17TH CENTURY)

LOUIS XV
(EARLY TO MIDDLE
18TH CENTURY)

LOUIS XVII
(LATE 18TH CENTURY)

DIRECTOIRE AND EMPIRE
(EARLY 19TH CENTURY)

AMERICAN COLONIAL
(18TH CENTURY)

AMERICAN FEDERAL
(EARLY 19TH CENTURY)

FRENCH PROVINCIAL

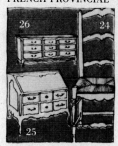

EARLY AMERICAN

SCANDINAVIAN

MEDITERRANEAN

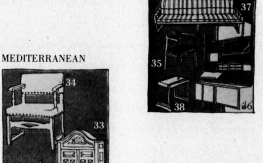

ORIENTAL

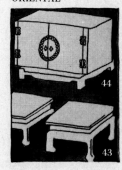

INTERNATIONAL

best in furniture design withstood the test of time and become our heritage from the past. Many of the European traditional styles that have survived are named after the monarchs in whose reign they were created. For centuries, royalty influenced all the arts and controlled the purse strings, and only the titled upper classes could afford the work of great craftsmen whose designs are being mass-produced today. Whether ornate or simple, traditional furniture displays excellence of proportion and attention to detail. Moderately priced reproductions now available are:

ENGLISH FURNITURE OF THE 18TH AND 19TH CENTURIES

Queen Anne (early 18th century). Because it is small in scale, well proportioned, and has only a moderate amount of carving and embellishment, Queen Anne furniture is well suited to the contemporary American home. Characteristics are the cabriole or curved leg, often on a claw-and-ball foot; the scallop shell motif; and splat-back chairs with curved top rails. Tall highboys were popular and the variety of occasional tables includes the folding card table and the small, round tilt-top with piecrust edge. 1. Curved splat-back chair. 2. Queen Anne small sofa. 3. Queen Anne lowboy.

Chippendale (middle 18th century). The use of exquisite carving as decoration on furniture reached its height during this period under the leadership of Thomas Chippendale, a cabinetmaker of extraordinary skill. He topped highboys and secretaries with graceful curved pediments and adorned chair backs with ribbon and bow carvings, the latter reflecting a French influence. The Chippendale camelback sofa and wing chair take an Oriental turn in the use of straight, square legs, sometimes with fretwork designs. He also retained the cabriole leg and claw-and-ball foot of the preceding Queen Anne period. Mahogany was the favored wood because it lent itself so well to carving. 4. Chair with carved splat. 5. Camelback sofa. 6. Secretary with broken pediment.

Adam (late 18th century). The discovery at this time of the ruins of Pompeii brought about a revival of classic design in English cabinetry. Couple this with the fact that the Adam brothers were architects as well as cabinetmakers, and you have the appearance of classic architectural details on furniture—urns, egg and dart moldings, acanthus leaves, and legs shaped like classic columns. Straight lines predominated, relieved by tapered legs and a penchant for oval chair backs. Mahogany remained the choice in wood. Although much admired and appreciated today, Adam furniture is perhaps too formal for widespread popularity in contemporary America. 7. Adam chair with lozenge back motif.

Hepplewhite (late 18th and early 19th centuries). Following the Adam tradition, George Hepplewhite produced a style of elegance and classic purity. He was fond of shield or oval backs on chairs, tambour doors on cabinets, and rosettes or medallions as embellishment. An important change at this time was the emphasis on chests of drawers and long, low sideboards rather than highboys. 8. Shield-back chair. 9. Serpentine front sideboard.

Sheraton (late 18th and early 19th centuries). Also a disciple of the Adam brothers, Thomas Sheraton favored a graceful, lightly scaled look in furniture. He saw beauty as inherent in fine cabinet woods, particularly mahogany, and, therefore, leaned toward inlays rather than carving as decoration. His sideboards have slightly curving fronts and tapered legs. 10. Spindle-arm sofa. 11. A Sheraton pedestal table.

FRENCH FURNITURE OF THE 17TH, 18TH, AND 19TH CENTURIES

Louis XIV (late 17th century). The lavishness of French Court life under the great, luxury-loving French king is reflected in the heavy, massive, baroque furniture designed under Louis XIV. Hardly the thing for a honeymoon cottage, this style abounds in curves, carving, gilding, and inlays of ivory, mother-of-pearl, and brass. Upholstery fabrics include lush velvets, tapestries, and damasks. Today, Louis XIV antiques or reproductions are most apt to be found as occasional accent pieces in rooms that feature traditional furniture. 12. Carved and decorated chair.

Louis XV (early to middle 18th century). While still richly embellished, Louis XV furniture is smaller and more delicate in scale than that of the earlier king. Important is the fact that designs at this time were being influenced by women close to the king, most notable were Mesdames de Pompadour and Du Barry. Pleasing femininity is evident in small writing desks, chaise longues, and occasional tables. Ornamentation takes the form of musical themes, flowers and ribbons, gold lacquer, colored marble. Fabrics: damask, chintz, and printed linen. 13. Painted chair. 14. Bombe commode.

Louis XVI (late 18th century). Like neighboring European countries, France went along with the return to classicism that followed the rediscovery of Pompeii. Furniture remained rich and elegant, but straight lines replaced curves and classic symbols reappeared. Rosettes, ribbons and beads, fluting, and reeding were used as decoration. In fabrics, striped satins and pleasant toile patterns prevailed. 15. A chair with fluted leg.

Directoire and Empire (early 19th century). For a brief transitional period after the revolution, the French Directoire ruled not only the government, but also the arts. Reacting against the excesses of the past monarchs, the Directoire insisted upon severe, straight-lined furniture relieved by classic or military emblems. But the ill-fated Directoire was soon overthrown by

Napoleon. While continuing in the Greek neoclassic tradition, design of the Empire period reflects Napoleon's own personality. Furniture became more massive in scale with square legs, claw feet, and heavy bases, the latter sometimes columnar or ornamented with caryatids. Acanthus leaves, scrolls, and honeysuckle are prevalent. The emperor's military achievements are symbolized in eagles, torches, crossed swords and the letter "N" surrounded by a laurel wreath. 16. Directoire chair. 17. Empire table with caryatid motif.

AMERICAN FURNITURE OF THE 18TH AND 19TH CENTURIES

American Colonial (18th century). The more prosperous American colonists rejected the designs of local cabinetmakers and imported furniture from England. Native craftsmen began to copy the work of the Queen Anne, Chippendale, and Sheraton periods. Though differing in details and materials, the reproductions were very faithful to the originals in proportions, design, and quality of workmanship. Primarily turned out in the cities, American Colonial furniture was traditional rather than provincial in feeling. Today, American Colonial furniture of the true Queen Anne and Chippendale schools is much in demand. 18. Chippendale-type wing chair. 19. Queen Anne-type tea table. 20. Queen Anne-type Colonial flattop highboy.

American Federal (early 19th century). Their freedom won, the American people wanted to stand on their own feet artistically as well as politically. This was expressed, symbolically, in a profusion of American eagles adorning everything from furniture to fabrics. Duncan Phyfe, famed cabinetmaker and trend-setter of the Federal period, led the gradual shift away from the Sheraton/Hepplewhite influence into the Directoire and Empire mold of postrevolutionary France. While it was inevitable that America would break its cultural ties with Britain and feel more kinship with the French, Phyfe's work suffered from the change. He is best known for his lyre-back chairs, pedestal tables, and sofa with curved base, flared legs, and lion's paw feet. 21. Sofa with scroll arm. 22. Pedestal dining table. 23. Lyre-back chair.

Provincial

Provincial furniture, the proud offspring of traditional design, represents the attempts of local cabinetmakers in the provinces to copy the court furniture of their day. In much the same way as budget-price dress manufacturers work with expensive originals, they adapted classic designs to the requirements of the masses and their own limitations in tools, talents, and materials. Provincial furniture is usually smaller in scale than the original to suit the more modest homes of the lower classes, and minus some of the carving and other intricate details. These factors also make it cheaper to reproduce today. While no expense was spared by the upper classes to secure the finest, often the rarest, woods and fabrics from every accessible part of the world, cabinetmakers who served the general public improvised with whatever was cheap and readily available at home, substituting pine for hardwoods, cotton for silks, etc. Provincial furniture is a very adaptable style that is well suited to the generally smaller room sizes of modern housing. Also, you can coordinate provincial styles with all other items of home furnishings, such as wallcoverings, floor coverings, and accessories. Popularly priced current furniture favorites are:

French Provincial. The provincial furniture of France that attracts such a wide following today is primarily derived from the carved, curved, and colorful designs of Louis XV. Curved legs, painted finishes, bombe drawer fronts, and an overall femininity in feeling are retained, but in greatly simplified versions of the original. Today French provincial attracts a wide following because it reflects the grace and charm of the past yet it looks young and fresh and is small in scale to suit modern interiors. 24. Ladder-back chair. 25. Slant-front desk. 26. Curve-front dresser.

Early American. The vigorous, spartan life in the American pioneer manifested itself in furniture that was simple, small-scale, hardy, and practical—usually made of oak, maple, or pine. Early American is characterized by straight lines, small and plain hardware, turned legs, spindle- or ladder-back chairs and rockers, rush seats, and harvest or drop-leaf tables. Open cupboards, hutches, and plate racks feature sides cut in a simple pattern of curves. Chests and chairs are often painted in provincial floral motifs, a colorful innovation of the Pennsylvania Dutch settlers. The Shakers, a religious sect, introduced a severely simple kind of furniture devoid of decoration, similar to twentieth-century modern. 27. Ladder-back, rush seat. 28. Hitchcock chair, stenciled back. 29. Bow-back Windsor chair. 30. Buffet with open hutch. 31. An Early American dry sink.

Mediterranean. Actually, the style we refer to as Mediterranean is primarily Spanish or Mexican. The Spanish flavor in furniture is based on a heavy, structural look—block-front cabinets, much carving, massive straight-legged chairs with plush velvet or leather seats, and tables with curving wrought iron bases. Perhaps more important is the background that goes with this setting—wrought iron lamps and ornaments, colored tiles, rough-hewn ceiling beams, stucco textured walls, and other Moorish architectural and accessory details. 32. Table with curved wrought iron base. 33. Block-front secretary. 34. Velvet-covered chair, nailhead trim.

Contemporary or Modern

Contemporary or modern furniture (you will find these terms used interchangeably) is the twentieth century's answer to the need for a design form more representative of the vast changes that have taken place in our way of life. Inspired by modern architecture and technology, it is a no-nonsense type of design in which the emphasis is on function and all unnecessary embellishment is stripped away. Chairs molded out of plastic and supported on steel, entire walls lined with built-in furniture, and the use of geometric design forms are among the results of a striving to create a total look in which furniture becomes one with its environment.

Scandinavian. The Scandinavians are masters of the art of making wood (walnut, teak, or birch in oil finishes) look beautiful in itself. Cabinets are utterly simple, without decoration. There are entire walls of built-in storage shelves, cabinets, desks, dining tables. Steam bending gives beautiful, sculptured curves to wood parts of chairs and sofas. Upholstery fabrics are tweeds, textures of modern prints. Tables nest to save floor space. 35. Captain's chair, steambent curve. 36. Wall-hung unit. 37. Sleigh-base sofa. 38. Nest of tables.

International. Much of the modern furniture being made in America must be credited to a movement that started after World War I at the German Bauhaus school, an international gathering place for progressive designers. Its disciples related furniture to architecture, believed that "form follows function," and used the architect's materials—plastics, glass, and metal. Classics of this school are the free-flowing molded plastic pedestal table and chairs of Eero Saarinen, the molded plywood and leather contoured lounge chair of Charles Eames, and the Barcelona group of Mies van der Rohe. The latter, introduced in 1929, at the

Barcelona Fair, includes leather chairs and glass-topped, steel-based tables. 39. Eames wood and leather chair. 40. Saarinen pedestal table. 41. Van der Rohe steel and glass table, and 42. his Barcelona chair.

Oriental. Reacting against the clutter of Victorian and seeking relief from the pressures of modern living, America turned to the Orient—particularly Japan. Sliding shoji screens instead of walls, tatami mats on bare wood floors, low tables in smooth lacquer finishes, paper lanterns, and graceful flower arrangements—all these bring light, air, and spaciousness indoors. American-made furniture of Oriental influence includes low-slung upholstery groups, often in rattan or wood with turnings that simulate bamboo, very low cocktail tables, and simple, rectangular cabinets ornamented with brass hardware. 43. Low snack table/stool. 44. Lacquered cabinet with brass hardware.

Glossary of Furniture Terms

ANTIQUE: recent United States customs law designates objects made one hundred years ago as antiques. *ANTIQUING:* finish applied to furniture to simulate the soft, worn appearance that normally comes with age. *APRON:* decorative strip of wood or other material that connects table or chair legs. *ARMOIRE:* large, high, and usually very decorative wardrobe cabinet. *BANQUETTE:* upholstered bench for seating two or more, usually in a breakfast nook or dinette. *BAROQUE:* richly ornamented and not in the classic tradition. *BERGERE:* large, upholstered armchair in French traditional style. *BOMBE:* swelling curve applied to some traditional cabinet fronts. *BREAKFRONT:* large, high storage piece consisting of a base cabinet topped by an enclosed shelf unit. *BURL:* decorative wood veneer with knotlike pattern. *CABRIOLE:* graceful, curved leg, usually with ornamented foot, associated with Queen Anne and Chippendale periods. *CASE:* trade name for storage furniture as distinguished from upholstery. *CHAISE LONGUE:* chair with a long seat providing a leg rest. *CHINOISERIE:* painted decoration in the Chinese manner. *CLAW-AND-BALL FOOT:* lion's paw grasping a ball used as a decorative motif on traditional curved legs. *CLASSICAL:* adhering to traditional design forms, particularly those of Roman or Greek heritage. *COMMODE:* small cabinet, used as a washstand in the pitcher-and-bowl era, now popular as a nightstand or chest. *CONSOLE TABLE:* space-saving table affixed to the wall with brackets. *CLUB CHAIR:* small-scale upholstered armchair. *COMB-BACK:* Windsor chair with top rail and spindles resembling a woman's decorative comb. *DISTRESSED:* furniture finish pitted and marked to simulate the effects of age. *DOVETAIL:* furniture joint in which two pieces of wood interlock without nails or other hardware. *DOWEL:* small, round peg of wood that joins two wood furniture parts by fitting into holes. *FILIGREE:* lacy, decorative metalwork on furniture. *FINIAL:* tip of an ornamental pinnacle, as the decorative carved pineapples topping some poster beds, or the top of a lamp. *GATELEG:* drop-leaf table with legs that swing out for support when leaves are in use. *GALLERY:* decorative top rail around a table or shelf. *HARDWOOD:* firm, hard woods used in furniture making—cherry, oak, maple, mahogany, walnut, and others. *HARVEST TABLE:* long, narrow drop-leaf dining table originally used in farmhouse kitchens. *HITCHCOCK:* Early American chair maker whose name is given to wood chair with curved top rail, painted and stenciled finish. *HUTCH:* open storage unit forming the top part of a buffet/hutch combination. *INLAY:* layer of wood veneer or other material set in a cabinet or table surface for decorative effect. *LADDER-BACK:* provincial chair with horizontal rungs across the back. *LACQUER FINISH:* protective coating of resin that gives a glossy finish to furniture. *LAMINATED PLASTIC:* layer of hard plastic bonded to a wood base. *LOWBOY:* low chest of drawers. *MARQUETRY:* inlay pattern of different woods or other materials. *MODULAR:* standard in size, referring to furniture units of the same height and width that may be stacked or placed next to each other. *NEOCLASSIC:* revival of the classic influence in furniture design. *OIL FINISHED:* rubbed with oil to impart a soft sheen rather than a glossy furniture finish. *ORMOLU:* imitation gold hardware or decoration. *PATINA:* soft, mellow finish that comes to wood or metal through age and normal usage. *PEDESTAL TABLE:* supported by a column or base rather than legs. *PEDIMENT:* decoration over doorways. Also used atop traditional highboys, particularly in form of broken pediment—two slanted S-curves facing each other. *PIECRUST TABLE:* small, round pedestal table with fluted edge resembling a piecrust. *ROCOCO:* originally an eighteenth-century decorative style, the word now refers to anything lavishly ornamented. *RUSH SEAT:* woven straw seat used much in Early America. *SERPENTINE:* S-curve shape used on buffets and other traditional cabinets. *SIDE CHAIR:* armless chair, usually part of a dining group. *STENCILED:* decorating by painting through a perforated pattern. *STRETCHER:* wood or metal strips connecting furniture legs. *TESTER:* four-poster bed fitted with canopy frame. *TILT-TOP:* space-saving table with top that tilts to vertical position when not in use. *TRESTLE:* table base in which a decorative horizontal stretcher is joined to two vertical side pieces. *TRUNDLE:* space-saving twin beds in which one slides under the other when not in use. *VENEER:* thin, top layer of wood, usually of fine quality, placed over layers of a cheaper wood. This technique gives strength to flat furniture surfaces and permits use of decorative inlays. *WEBBING:* interwoven strips of strong plastic or other materials that are used to form outdoor furniture seats or give support to all other upholstered seating. *WELTING:* the seamed border visible around edges of upholstery cushions. *WING CHAIR:* an upholstered chair with decorative side pieces flanking its high back.

Chapter 4
Making Floor Plans
for Each Room

t last, you've found the right apartment—and your plans for the future can really begin to take shape. Now that you know exactly how much living space you will have, you can stop thinking in generalities and get down to specifics. How can you utilize the space you've just leased to best advantage? By drawing up a floor plan for each room and adding some imagination and vision, it's possible to get a pretty good picture in mind of how an apartment will look when furnished.

Ideally, floor plans should be made before doing any furniture shopping, since it is the dimensions of the room that determine how much furniture will fit in and which sizes are most suitable. If you already have some pieces you plan to use, start by putting them in position and then working around them.

Floor plans may take a little time, but they can save you money and prevent the agony that often results when you rely on your eye

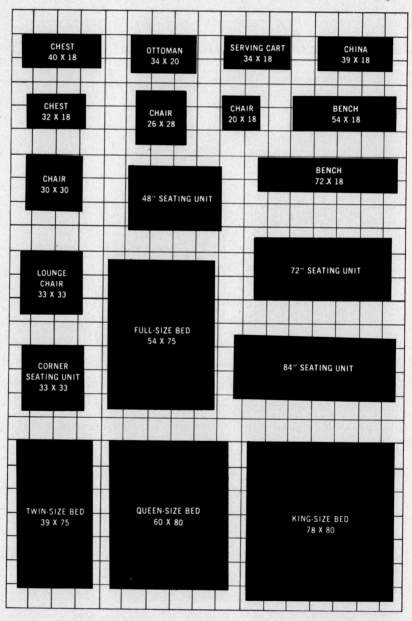

CHEST
40 X 18

OTTOMAN
34 X 20

SERVING CART
34 X 18

CHINA
39 X 18

CHEST
32 X 18

CHAIR
26 X 28

CHAIR
20 X 18

BENCH
54 X 18

CHAIR
30 X 30

48" SEATING UNIT

BENCH
72 X 18

LOUNGE
CHAIR
33 X 33

72" SEATING UNIT

FULL-SIZE BED
54 X 75

CORNER
SEATING UNIT
33 X 33

84" SEATING UNIT

TWIN-SIZE BED
39 X 75

QUEEN-SIZE BED
60 X 80

KING-SIZE BED
78 X 80

to Typical Furniture Pieces

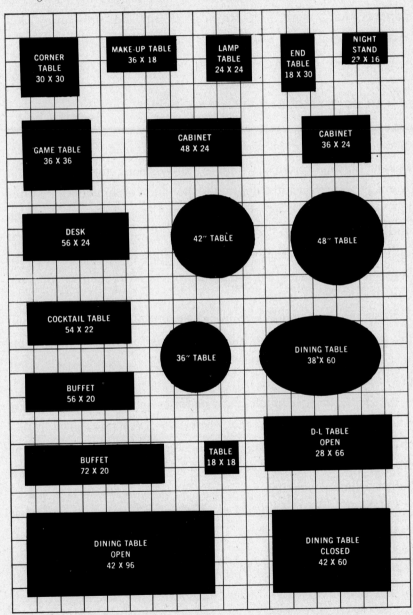

rather than a yardstick. In an hour's time, you can rearrange the furniture ten times without lifting anything heavier than a piece of paper. What's more, you can crumple up and throw away your mistakes, then make a fresh start with a different selection.

How to Make a Floor Plan

Measure everything in sight to the quarter inch. Include walls, beams, jutting corners, windows, sills, doors, radiators, floors. Know the length, width, depth plus height of architectural features and stationary objects. Using preruled graph paper, draw an outline of the room to a scale of ¼ inch equals one foot. Then indicate all doors, windows, beams, fireplaces, etc. Make several copies of this plan so that you can work out different arrangements and decide which is best.

Basic furniture you think you will need should go on a list. Note the function that must be fulfilled by this furniture—seating for six, dining for four, bookshelves for all of your books plus other possessions, and so on.

Utilize furniture templates representing typical pieces, drawn to a scale of ¼ inch equals one foot. Trace the templates shown in this chapter or have these pages duplicated at your local library or other places that offer photo copying services, then glue them to a light cardboard backing.

Electrical outlets should be marked on the floor plan. Then list items to be serviced by them. If extra outlets are needed, find out how much this will cost.

Place cut-outs on the floor plan. Keep in mind logical placement for the room's activities. Allow for traffic patterns. Be sure each seating area can be lighted adequately and is near a table.

Strive for balance. Consider the scale of pieces in relation to each other and the whole room. Don't cram big pieces into small areas or treat large areas too sparsely.

Be prepared to change. Perhaps the pieces of furniture you plan on acquiring just don't seem to work. If there isn't enough room, consider substitutions that save space, such as dual-purpose or wall-hung furniture.

Make a rough sketch. When you find a workable floor plan, either paste down your templates or trace outlines of them on the graph paper. If you are pleased with the result, buy only what fits this plan.

Hints on Planning a Living Room

Such a variety of activities take place in the living room, from quiet relaxation for two to entertaining groups of people, that there is plenty of strategy to be used in order to make the most attractive and practical use of available space.

When planning "traffic areas" a good rule to follow is to allow at least two feet of unobstructed space wherever passage is necessary. Even more width is desirable in spaces like foyers and hallways. If you have a narrow hall, it is better to leave the area free, relying on wall-hung accessories or an interesting wallpaper pattern for decorative interest, than to clutter it with furniture.

Where the view from living room windows is interesting, you may wish to place seating pieces to take advantage of it. If the view has no merit, you might concentrate instead on a conversation grouping with seating arranged so that a number of people can face each other. Such a grouping could include a cocktail table, end tables, or even chests beside chairs.

A fireplace often dictates the arrangement, with a sofa facing the hearth and chairs grouped at the sides, or sofas and love seats extending at right angles from the wall.

In a small room, furniture placed against the wall saves interior space. Keep in mind, however, that all furniture should not be lined up along the walls. For greater interest, place at least one piece, perhaps a table desk, so that it extends out from the wall.

For a pleasing overall feeling, do not put all your best pieces in one area, but distribute them throughout the room. A good piece will attract the eye and at the same time distract your eye from a lesser piece that must be included for function. Distribute "weight" so that all bulky feeling furnishings are not in one area and all light pieces in another.

When placing a large, tall, or important piece against the wall —cabinet or breakfront displaying art objects and books—do not confuse the visual appeal of the piece by placing too many other pieces around or near it. Let this one selection be a focal point.

If either of you has a hobby, attends college, or brings work home from the office, special furniture and lighting may be called for—a cozy corner with a well-lighted desk or table, a large surface for cutting out dress patterns, a place for a music stand or for an artist's easel.

DUAL-PURPOSE AREAS

Space is very expensive, so it pays to make the most of it. If your living room is too small to accommodate a dining area without looking cluttered, or you're not ready to buy a dining table and chairs, a cocktail table that rises to dining height may be perfect. You may need a sofa that converts to a single or double bed, end tables with space for linen storage, dining chairs comfortable and attractive enough to seat guests in the living room, or chairs and

tables on casters that may be shifted around when needed.

Floor Plans for Bedrooms

The most important single piece of furniture in a bedroom is, of course, the bed itself. The first step is to decide on a size and type, then figure out where you are going to put it and arrange other furniture accordingly. A very popular size is the 60″ x 80″ queen, but if you have the space, do consider the luxury of the 78″ x 80″ king, affording the same roominess as a pair of twin beds. The standard double size, 54″ x 75″, is no longer adequate for the tallest generation of Americans on record. Remember, either a queen- or king-size mattress can be worked into the floor plan of an average room, about 12′ x 15′.

ALTERNATE TYPES OF BEDS

Aside from the conventional mattress and boxspring arrangement, there are several alternate bed types that might be suitable to your special needs.

Folding, for storing away out of sight in the daytime. Several versions fold out of a cupboard or doorway.

Four-poster, with or without a canopy, for a really impressive, traditional look.

Hanging bed, rigged from the ceiling to save space. This should be installed by a builder.

Platform bed, for a very modern and tailored look, a mattress is placed on a platform. If the platform is larger than the mattress, it will provide a seating ledge all around that can double as a built-in night table.

Sofa bed, the perfect solution for sleeping and seating when space is limited. If you do decide to use the sleep sofa frequently, consider investing in a very good mattress for comfort and for greater longevity.

Water bed, said to be very comfortable and provide a great night's sleep. It can be noisy, unless all air bubbles are pressed out and should be heated since the water tends to draw out body heat. Since it weighs about half a ton when filled, be certain to check with the landlord before buying one to be sure he will allow it in the building.

For those who love to sit and read or watch television in bed, a headboard is an absolute must for back support. A padded headboard is the most comfortable and can be given a custom look with fabric or sheeting to match the bedspread. If, however, a headboard in your bedroom is just for decorative effect, you may decide that a framed graphic or painting will also give the effect you want.

MAKING BEDROOMS MORE USEFUL

Properly equipped with a few extras, a bedroom is ideal as a second living room. Try to find a spot for one or two comfortable chairs or even a small table for playing cards or serving snacks.

For storage, the most efficient method is to have an entire wall system of drawers, cabinets, and shelves of varying sizes. If you prefer a bedroom set (dresser, chest, night tables), try to avoid the stereotyped look of having everything match. You can vary textures by having one or two pieces in materials other than wood—a cane headboard, rattan blanket chest, or wicker chair. A change of pace in wood finishes also makes for interest—one painted and decorated accent piece, perhaps, or an antique rocking chair.

Be sure the storage pieces you choose suit available wall space. High, narrow chests may be best in a small room with wall space interrupted by multiple doors and windows. In other situations, one or two long pieces or a series of units that go side by side would be more efficient.

Don't forget to consider the closet as part of the room when deciding how much storage furniture is necessary. If the closet is large enough, have it fitted with racks and shelves for handbags, shirts, sweaters, and other accessories. If closet space is limited or there is no linen closet in the apartment, an extra piece of furniture or armoire may be desirable. You might also buy drawers on casters that slide under the bed for out-of-season clothing and extra linens. Be on the lookout for other "bonus" storage—night tables with cabinets, seating benches that are also blanket chests, and bookcase headboards.

Typical Floor Plans for Living, Dining, and Bedrooms

Rooms come in all shapes and sizes, some of them less perfect than others. On the pages that follow are suggested layouts for a variety of rooms typical of modern housing. Use them to stimulate your own thinking and work out the best possible arrangements for your own individual needs.

1. LIVING IN ONE ROOM

The one-room apartment, where facilities for dining, sleeping, entertaining, and relaxing share the same four walls, presents the greatest challenge of all. Because so much time is spent here, care must be taken to avoid monotony, overcrowding, and a boxed-in feeling. With so many good-looking sleep sofas now available, the aesthetic problem of disguising the bed no longer exists, but be sure to allow enough floor space for the opened mattress. Any furniture in the way should be lightweight or on casters. To vary the

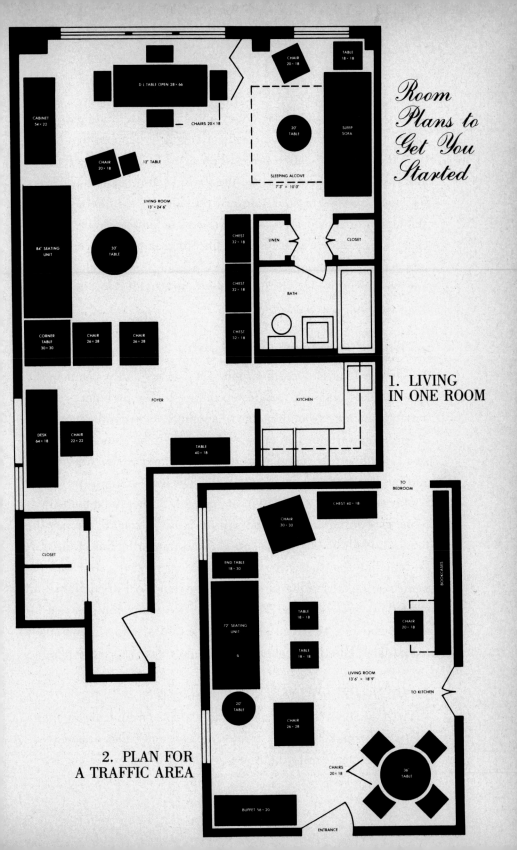

Room Plans to Get You Started

CABINET 54 × 22

D L TABLE OPEN 28 × 66

CHAIRS 20 × 18

CHAIR 20 · 18

TABLE 18 · 18

CHAIR 20 × 18

12" TABLE

LIVING ROOM 13' × 24'6"

20" TABLE

SLEEP SOFA

SLEEPING ALCOVE 7'3" × 10'0"

84" SEATING UNIT

30" TABLE

CHEST 32 · 18

LINEN

CLOSET

CHEST 32 · 18

BATH

CORNER TABLE 30 × 30

CHAIR 26 × 28

CHAIR 26 × 28

CHEST 32 · 18

FOYER

KITCHEN

1. LIVING IN ONE ROOM

DESK 64 · 18

CHAIR 22 · 22

TABLE 40 · 18

TO BEDROOM

CLOSET

CHEST 40 · 18

CHAIR 30 · 30

BOOKCASES

END TABLE 18 · 30

72" SEATING UNIT

TABLE 18 · 18

CHAIR 20 · 18

TABLE 18 · 18

LIVING ROOM 13'6" × 18'9"

TO KITCHEN

20" TABLE

CHAIR 26 · 28

2. PLAN FOR A TRAFFIC AREA

CHAIRS 20 · 18

36" TABLE

BUFFET 56 · 20

ENTRANCE

floor plan illustrated, use cube tables you can store pillows in rather than a coffee table, or have ottomans or benches that can be pulled around the coffee table when extra seating is needed. For still another arrangement, use the main seating area as the place for your sleep-sofa and convert the alcove to another use— television or music area, study corner, or dining alcove. In any case, use as much multifunction furniture as possible. Extension tables, pull-up chairs that double for dining, lightly scaled indoor/ outdoor furniture, see-through tables, and tables that nest—all are excellent space savers.

2. PLAN FOR A TRAFFIC AREA

When a long and narrow room also serves as the main traffic area, it takes planning to sidestep dullness. The problem is to free a path from one end of the room to another, yet avoid the monotony of lining up furniture on either side. In the plan shown, variety is sustained by using round as well as square and rectangular shapes and positioning them asymmetrically. The long-and-narrow look of bookcases is offset with a chair at one end. A chest next to the bedroom doorway and the round dining table diagonally across the room also help break up the straight-and-narrow feeling of the traffic lane between them. In planning a room yourself, start with the main seating area and arrange pieces so that the traffic pattern you want flows around them. Next, decide how many you can seat for dining and include extra chairs, stack tables, and serving space for parties. This plan could work in one room with a sleep-sofa.

3. L-SHAPE LIVING/DINING ROOM

The L-shape living and dining area seen so frequently in apartments and small homes is treated in a manner that allows maximum functionalism for both areas without overcrowding or inter-

Room Plans to Get You Started

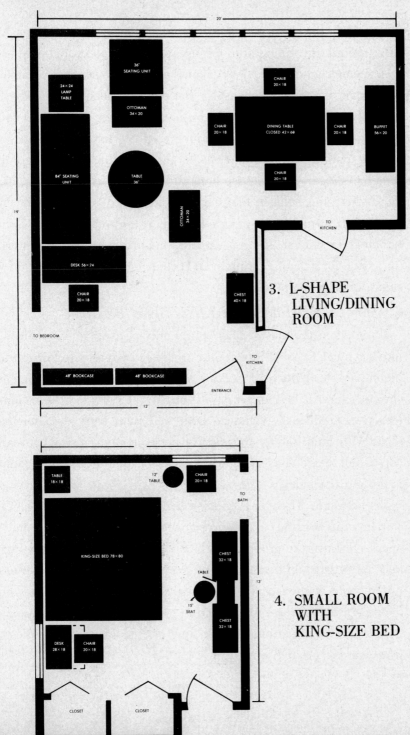

20'

36"
SEATING UNIT

24 × 24
LAMP
TABLE

OTTOMAN
34 × 20

CHAIR
20 × 18

CHAIR
20 × 18

DINING TABLE
CLOSED 42 × 60

CHAIR
20 × 18

BUFFET
56 × 20

84" SEATING
UNIT

TABLE
36"

OTTOMAN
34 × 20

CHAIR
20 × 18

DESK 56 × 24

19'

CHAIR
20 × 18

TO
KITCHEN

CHEST
40 × 18

3. L-SHAPE LIVING/DINING ROOM

TO BEDROOM

TO
KITCHEN

48" BOOKCASE

48" BOOKCASE

ENTRANCE

12'

TABLE
18 × 18

12"
TABLE

CHAIR
20 × 18

TO
BATH

KING-SIZE BED 78 × 80

CHEST
32 × 18

TABLE

15"
SEAT

13'

CHEST
32 × 18

4. SMALL ROOM WITH KING-SIZE BED

DESK
28 × 18

CHAIR
20 × 18

CLOSET

CLOSET

fering with the flow of traffic. Several dual-purpose pieces of furniture are incorporated in the living room—a desk that doubles as a second lamp table, desk chair that can also serve for dining, and a pair of ottomans on casters that can be wheeled about where needed for extra seating. In the dining area, where six persons can be accommodated at sit-down dinners, plans have been laid for serving buffets and brunches to larger gatherings—just regroup the chairs elsewhere and use both table and buffet as serving surfaces. Note the balance that has been achieved, with the heavier pieces of furniture distributed around the room rather than bunched in one area. This same arrangement would also work quite well for a couple living in an L-shape one-room apartment by substituting a sleep-sofa.

4. SMALL ROOM WITH KING-SIZE BED

Even when the master bedroom is only of average dimensions, like a typical 11' x 13' room plan, there is no reason to forego the incomparable luxury of a king-size bed. In the arrangement shown, every inch of space is well utilized to provide all the comforts you could ask—oversize bed, sufficient storage, a lounge chair with lamp table, and even a desk or study area. You can copy such space-conserving ideas as the use of a desk as a lamp table and the side-by-side grouping of twin chests with dressing table between. There are endless ways in which you can stack storage units together to conserve space and at the same time have one large furniture grouping to balance the bulk of the king-size bed and night table arrangement. Variations on the theme illustrated could be the use of twin storage chests as night tables to gain added drawer space and a triple dresser to replace the dressing table/chest combination. For an uncluttered look, fit the closet with drawers or shelves.

Chapter 5
Budget Decorating

ecorating on a budget calls for making compromises—but never with quality. It means putting your money where it does the most good and cutting corners only in places where you won't find that, in the long run, you haven't spent wisely. If you find yourselves short of cash, substitute other assets like imagination, artistic or manual skills you possess, or willingness to spend time as a substitute for money.

Expensive vs. Cheap

There is a time to buy the best and a time to look for a low price tag. Both have a place in your budget if you are thinking in terms of growing and gradually acquiring the quality home furnishings you will have for a very long time.

Suppose the bedroom furniture you want costs more than you have to spend right now. Instead of settling for a less expensive set you don't like as much and may never be happy with, why not choose just a few good basic pieces, then fill in with inexpensive items to complete the room and provide for your needs.

A good mattress and boxspring, plus whatever storage pieces you need, should be foremost on your list of priorities. The wall behind the bed can be decorated in any number of budget-wise ways to minimize your immediate need for a headboard—hang a large picture or colorful tapestry, drape fabric or sheeting for a canopy effect, or make an inexpensive headboard from plywood covered with sheeting or quilted fabric. Even a terrific patterned wallpaper or fabric on the wall will help give this important part of the room a decorative look.

Instead of night tables, try tables in the appropriate size skirted to the floor with fabric. You can pick up pedestals in secondhand stores and have plywood tops cut to size at a lumber yard. As for a chair, you can have an old one slipcovered or find a secondhand chair in a flea market or secondhand store. Don't forget the possibility of using indoor/outdoor furniture.

The same type of budgeting will also help you acquire your living room and dining room furniture. Rather than buying a whole roomful of "budget" pieces, invest in a few well-designed pieces that you love to set the mood of your room and then fill in with secondhand, refurnished, or refinished furniture and inexpensive fabrics you can gradually replace.

By following this system, you will always have a nucleus of fine furnishings that keeps growing into something worthwhile, rather than a lot of mediocre and "temporary" possessions you will want to get rid of, leaving you right back where you started.

Some couples, particularly if they don't plan on staying too long

at their present address, choose to put a lot of their money into buying good quality lamps, room-size and area rugs, a wall storage unit, and some occasional tables. For now, they make do with upholstered furniture and other items gleaned from any number of money-saving sources.

Take-Out Furniture

Labor is an expensive commodity reflected in the price of everything you buy. If you do some of the work yourself—assembling, finishing, and even carrying furniture home from the store yourselves—you are spending time and saving money. Here are several ways to spend less for furniture, some of which involve buying new merchandise and others that call for exploring the secondhand market.

Knockdown furniture comes in parts you can carry home and assemble yourself with a few simple hand tools. In one case, pillows are sold in handsome boxes. The boxes then become a platform for the seat and back cushions—and there you have an instant sofa. Another clever knockdown arrangement consists of chrome tubing that can be fitted together to form the structure for tables and a wall-storage system. Plywood cut to size makes the table tops and shelves. When you are ready to move, just disassemble the parts, repack them, and you're off.

Building supply stores and other furniture-in-parts stores across the country provide additional ideas in simple but attractive modern furniture. Pick out a flush door and a set of legs for a cocktail table. Sofas and love seats can be made with flush doors as bases and slipcovered foam slabs for the seats and backs. Years from now, when you are more permanently settled in your own home or a larger apartment, you may want to invest in the more formal look of conventional upholstered furniture for the living room. Your furniture-in-parts can then be moved to a family room.

Furniture-in-the-raw, from shelving to cabinets, also represents savings since you do the finishing yourself with wood stain, paint, or lacquer. Antiquing is an especially popular, easy way to give unfinished furniture the glamour treatment and add a colorful accent to a decorating scheme. For a real custom look, you can buy moldings and special hardware to turn a plain cabinet into one that looks Early American, French Provincial, Mediterranean, or traditional. Check out the showroom of a well-stocked lumber yard for additional ideas on decorating with wood moldings, shutters, hardware, and other trimmings.

The Secondhand Market

From thrift shops run by charitable organizations to used furniture and antique shops, searching for used furniture is a pleasant pastime that can be very worthwhile. Also worth investigating are flea markets, garage sales, country fairs, and auctions.

Generally, some labor is involved in restoring the treasures you acquire off the beaten path. If you get a good buy on wood furniture that needs to be stripped down and refinished, sending it to a commercial stripping shop may be well worth the cost. It will save hours of tedious effort and assures that your furniture will be stripped clean down to the bare wood, making it easy for you to achieve professional results when you stain it. The stripping shop will also tighten up loose joints and make other minor repairs for which you may not have the necessary tools or skills.

When buying used upholstery, avoid pieces with sagging or

popping springs, rickety legs, and other deficiencies that will require the services of a reupholsterer. This can prove more costly than a new purchase. Also steer clear of upholstered furniture with the telltale odor of must or mildew—it isn't going to disappear. Best buys are sofas and chairs in sound condition that need only slipcovering to make them like new. Check furniture carefully before buying. Damaged legs and stretchers or missing pieces of applied decoration can be expensive to repair, and more often than not, matching replacement parts cannot be found.

Aside from saving money, secondhand stores offer an opportunity to find unusual, one-of-a-kind accessories and accent pieces that will individualize your home. Old-fashioned pier mirrors, costumers, gold leaf picture frames, copper and brass pots, milk cans, butter churners, kitchen and farm implements, spinning wheels, wagon wheels, parts of wrought iron gates, and a thousand other treasures lurk in those trash piles, so bring your imagination with you.

Decorating with Fabrics

Colorful, patterned fabrics bring beauty by the yard into interiors and give your home a marvelous custom touch. An especially good buy are today's bed linens, far too pretty to limit to beds alone.

Utilizing sheets is one of the quickest and least expensive ways to decorate living rooms and bedrooms. Coordinated sheeting collections feature ruffled bed skirts, ruffled pillow shams, bed and bath accessories, bedspreads, coverlets, quilts, and so on. When sewing with sheets it is advisable not to launder them first, in order to retain the sizing from the manufacturing process that will act as a protective agent against soiling for decorative pillows

and other nonwashable items that you plan on making.

Here is what you get in bed linens by way of yardage measurements.

Twin flat sheet, 66″x104″ = about 5¼ yds. 36″ fabric
Double flat sheet, 81″x104″ = about 6½ yds. 36″ fabric
Queen flat sheet, 90″x110″ = about 7½ yds. 36″ fabric
King flat sheet, 108″x110″ = about 9⅛ yds. 36″ fabric
Regular case, 42″x36″ = about 1⅛ yds. 36″ fabric
King size case, 42″x46″ = about 1⅜ yds. 36″ fabric

For dreamy decorating, these are just some of the projects you can undertake.

Customize windows to match your bed. Make curtains or draperies with matching tiebacks. Laminate sheeting fabric to a simple window shade. An iron-on shade laminating kit can be purchased at notions counters to simplify the process. If you have window shutters with fabric panels, insert sheeting.

Make a canopy for a bed. Ruffled sheeting is especially pretty for this.

Make a padded headboard. Have a piece of plywood cut to size at a lumber yard, then pad it and staple sheeting in place. For a more luxurious effect, use a quilt.

Decorate pillows. Cover pillows with ruffled pillow shams that are perfect for a crisp, frilly effect.

Slipcover a sofa or chair. This works especially well for sofas made up of pillow and back cushions placed on a platform.

Skirt a round table. This is pretty in both living room and bedroom, especially when you team it with matching curtains and/or decorative pillows. You can also make a tablecloth for the dining room from sheeting.

Keeping Up with Decorating Trends

Since new products, designs, and patterns, and new ways to do things are constantly appearing on the home furnishings scene, the best and the brightest budget ideas are often the newest. Keep up with what is going on by subscribing to decorating magazines and checking newsstands for special editions of magazines covering specific areas of the home.

If you are looking for new and inexpensive window treatments, or the latest kitchen and bath ideas, or ways to add finishing touches to your living room, buy a magazine devoted exclusively to the subject. Scan the Sunday newspapers for sales on linens, curtains, rugs, and furniture to get the most for your money.

Chapter 6
Putting Colors and
Patterns Together

T he sky is the limit when it comes to putting together a color scheme! But remember that good color schemes are just as easy to carry through on a budget as they are to put together with unlimited funds. The same amount of money, give or take a few dollars, will buy the same number of gallons of paint, rolls of wallpaper, or yards of fabric whether you go for routine, dull combinations, or bright, stimulating effects with lots of color and pattern.

What You Should Know About Color

Working with color is the fun part of getting your house together. So don't get caught up on a lot of technicalities that might get in the way of your own enthusiasm and imagination. There are, however, a few guidelines to familiarize yourself with before attempting to put a color scheme together.

If you think of a color wheel it will be easier to understand which colors look good together and what effects they have. Equidistant on the wheel are the three primary colors—red, yellow, and blue. When two primaries are combined, the secondary colors result—orange, green, and violet. Then there is a third range, the intermediates, formed by combining one primary and one secondary color—yellowish orange, reddish orange, reddish purple, bluish purple, yellowish green, and bluish green.

The blue and green families are referred to as cool colors—they have a calm, soothing effect that goes well in bedrooms or other places for relaxation. Red and yellow and their derivatives are warm and stimulating—good for active rooms and cheerful to look at while working in the kitchen.

These are the twelve basic colors that form the wheel. By using them in varying amounts, hundreds of different tints and shades are possible. Add to this black, white, and neutrals, and you have all the ingredients that go into a color scheme.

Following are three basic schemes you can put together:

Monochromatic, or one-color, scheme. This subtle but effective method works especially well for people who have a favorite color, like blue or green. Choose the one you like best, then vary it with several different tints and shades from light to dark. Suppose you decide on blue for the bedroom. You could paint the walls blue or white with a blue tint. Find a floral bedspread with lots of blue in it. Add white curtains with blue trim and a rug or carpet in a shade somewhat deeper than the walls.

Related, or analagous, scheme. Very popular and easy to work out, this scheme is based on two colors next to each other on the wheel, like blue and green or red and orange. One of these colors should predominate—blue used in large amounts, for example, then green introduced as a secondary color.

Complementary, or opposite, scheme. Lively and dramatic, this represents the bold use of two colors directly opposite or nearly opposite each other on the wheel—blue and orange, red and green, or blue and red.

In using any of these formulas, don't overlook the important role played by black, white, and the neutrals that range from beige into brown. And don't forget that wood furniture and bare floors are part of the total effect.

A LESSON IN PROPORTION

It's not only which colors you combine that matters, but the proportions in which you use them. To achieve balance, don't use colors in equal proportions. Instead, let one color predominate on at least two-thirds of the room's surfaces, use a second color in smaller amounts, and wind up with just a dash of a third color for accent. Usually, the predominant color is a neutral or light color used on about two-thirds of the room's surfaces, the second color is somewhat stronger, and the accent color is a vivid, but not overwhelming, attention-getter.

One of the simplest ways to make sure your colors go together and that you are using them in proper proportions is to collect fabric swatches, paint chips, and wallpaper patterns, then use them in conjunction with your floor plans, as explained in the previous chapter. If you have made three-dimensional floor plans, so much the better. Color in the walls with crayon to approximate your choice of paint, or paste a piece of wallpaper in place to help your vision. Then cut out swatches for upholstery fabrics, curtains, and other important items in sizes that relate to the way they will be used—the sofa swatch about three times as large as the coordinating upholstered chair, the rug sample larger, and so on. By spreading these out in front of your room plan, or actually cutting them to size and putting them in place, you can visualize the total effect quite easily. When shopping, take both floor plans and swatches with you rather than attempting to coordinate colors from memory. If possible, don't buy anything until all your samples are together and you've seen how well your plan is going to work.

What You Should Know About Pattern

An integral part of your color scheme is the pattern that goes with it. While one pattern per room used to be the rule, this generation is daring enough to follow the lead of professional decorators in using two or more patterns together, such as the vogue for pattern-on-pattern that is popular today. Influences from the Orient and other colorful geographic areas affect the use of multipattern and multicolors in a single room. These can be harmonious and tastefully combined by following the technique of the original designers and craftsmen.

Hard and fast rules don't exist. But generally, one floral and one geometric look well together when related by color—a pink floral on a white background, for example, teams well with a stripe in the same pink and white. A large floral also teams with a similar but smaller-in-scale floral. If you are new at the game, the best way to coordinate patterns is by seeking out correlated collections in the stores put together by famous designers.

When working with pattern swatches, remember that bold, intense patterns will be more so in larger amounts. The same goes for color—the small paint chip of an intense color will be more intense when you see it on the wall.

Where to Get Ideas

Indoors and out, it's a great big colorful world we live in, and you have only to look around you to find inspiration. The following are excellent sources of help:

Pick your colors from a pattern you like. An interesting wallpaper or fabric pattern provides a marvelous jumping off place for a color scheme because it clues you in not only to colors that go together, but the proportions in which to use them. If you are working with a floral wallpaper on a neutral or white background, use a color from the pattern on one wall and paint the other three to pick up the background color. Then pick up two more colors in the pattern. It's wise to be selective when working with a multicolor pattern, limiting yourselves to only the color you like best. Sheets and towels, available in every conceivable combination of colors and patterns, are a marvelous source of inspiration and can be used as curtains and slipcovers. Be sure to take a trip through the linen department when looking for ideas.

Work from a painting or tapestry you happen to love. A beautiful painting, perhaps a modern work of art that derives its merit solely from the use of color and form, can be both the focal point of a room and the inspiration for a wonderful color scheme. Other impressive wall hangings, even one you have done yourself and are proud of, are also excellent sources and will give your decorating scheme and your color scheme a highly individualized look.

Be guided by a model room setting. Zero in on one you've seen in a store or exhibit or a photograph from a magazine. This is a very sensible idea because the proportions of one color to another have already been worked out by a professional. You'll make substitutions, of course, selecting different patterns and tonal values to suit your own taste—but you'll be working from a model of proven effectiveness, thus eliminating second-guessing.

Start with a neutral or black and white background. Then play one or two colors against it. The beauty of this scheme is that your go-with-everything background will adapt easily to change should you tire of your present combination.

What Color Can Do

Among the most intriguing aspects of color are the optical and psychological illusions you can produce from its proper use. Here are some of them.

Make a small room seem larger. White or light colors recede, giving the effect of pushing the walls back in a room you wish were larger. Conversely, you can achieve a cozier effect in a large room by bringing the walls forward with intense color or a vivid pattern.

Change the shape of an imperfectly proportioned room. If the rooms in your apartment are too long and narrow, you can change the shape of them with color. Painting the two end walls in a deeper color will bring them forward, making the room appear narrower and wider. This trick works on ceilings as well—use white or light paint on a ceiling that is too low, and darker paints or patterned wallpaper to visually bring down a high ceiling.

Minimize architectural defects. Older buildings often have radiators, exposed pipes, unattractive window frames, and other architectural defects. To minimize these and make the wall look more unified, paint the pipes, window frames, or whatever else obtrudes in the same color as the wall. If it's a piece of furniture that bothers you—an overstuffed sofa, chair or chest that seems to stand out too much—slipcover or paint it the same color so that it will seem to blend into the wall. Conversely, use contrasting paint or stain to make the most of attractive moldings, window frames, and other good features already present.

Compensate for too much or too little natural light. Rooms that seem either cold or dreary because too little sunlight comes in take well to sunshine yellow, orange, and other warm colors. If the room gets plenty of light, blue and green are good choices to tone it down and make it seem cooler in hot weather.

SUMMING UP

As a final word of advice, don't limit yourself by being overly cautious in your approach to color coordination. You needn't try to match everything perfectly—sofa pillows are more interesting accessories when they are a shade lighter or darker than your rug, and the pink in your bedspread can be teamed with deeper shades of pink in other objects. Just as a tree becomes more beautiful when its leaves take on a dozen different hues, so can your home be more enchanting when you liven it up with varied color tones.

Chapter 7
Backgrounds and Finishing Touches

he total impact of your decorating scheme depends a lot on what you do with walls, wall-hung accessories, windows, and the small accessory touches that are so very personally yours. Walls take up so much space that they are worth considering for their decorative as well as functional value.

Painting Your Walls

Generally, the least expensive way to change the look or mood in a room is with a fresh coat of paint.

Applying white or off-white paint to all four walls is dramatic if you have a lot of color and pattern contrast elsewhere in the room.

Combining three walls of white or neutral paint with one wall in a color is effective if you want wall interest.

A rough-textured stucco effect or stained wood beams and molding strips applied in the style of Tudor houses are other ways of using white paint dramatically.

Papering Your Walls

The easiest way to decorate walls is to use patterned or textured wallcoverings—available at all price levels.

Natural texture effects —wallcoverings that look like grasscloth, burlap, cane, and bamboo—can be relied upon in situations where paint would do too little and a busy pattern would add too much. They provide relief from the overly smooth and precise look of Sheetrock and other architecturally bland walls.

Florals have a fresh look appropriate almost anywhere. There are neat small repeat patterns that suit provincial rooms, larger and more imposing blossoms for traditional settings, and stylized or abstract interpretations for contemporary rooms.

Geometrics, a very important group, take in such classics as stripes that suit either modern or formal period decor, and checks and plaids to enhance provincial or simple modern rooms. Then there are grille and scrollwork designs, a good companion for period furniture. For added excitement, there is the boldness of polka dots or squares and circles that create optical illusions.

Damasks, a stylized floral motif, belong to rooms where a rich, elegant look is sought.

Documentaries, patterns with a nostalgic or historic significance, can be a perfect finishing touch in rooms devoted to a particular period. French toiles, depicting pleasant country scenes, and Early American memorabilia are popular.

Wallpaper murals and scenics create a certain mood, perhaps a

French or Italian scene to give a continental look to a dining area. Scenics are often useful for providing an optical illusion of depth in a small area. They look best on a single wall or part of a wall with companion papers and borders filling out the surrounding area.

If you can measure, paste, and cut, you can hang most wallpapers yourselves, although heavy papers and foils are best left to experts. Obtain complete instructions and materials for the paper you are using from your wallpaper dealer. If your landlord says no to wallpaper, inquire about the peel and stick kind that can be zipped off when moving.

Wall-Hung Accessories

Accessories do much for a home, particularly when you combine paintings, prints, tapestries, and other framed art with three-dimensional objects like clocks, barometers, wood and metal sculptures, mirrors, sconces, planters, and standing objects placed on shelves.

If you don't have enough wall decor, add framed prints, old maps, and reproductions of paintings you can purchase inexpensively at museums, department and book stores. Old books and magazines often yield interesting photographs and even advertisements of quaint products that add charm.

Choose the right frame for the type picture: a simple, country style for fruit and floral prints or primitives; a more elaborate traditional frame in metal, gold leaf, or wood for formal subject matter; and a modern frame for bold twentieth-century art.

The frame should focus attention on the picture and draw the eye to the center of interest in the subject.

Select a frame that harmonizes in color and weight with the subject matter of the picture so they complement each other.

Be sure the frame does not dominate the picture. This sometimes happens when the art is in a light or delicate mood.

How you arrange pictures plus art objects is important. First, place your selections on the floor in an area equivalent to the wall space you plan to fill. Move them around until you are satisfied with the arrangement. Measure carefully before you start hammering. A single picture should be at eye level for a person of average height standing in the center of a room.

Window Treatments

Depending on where you live and what type windows you have, you may be able to satisfy both decorative and practical needs with one or two coverings for each window.

For affording privacy, controlling light and ventilation, there are venetian blinds, vertical blinds, and shutters. These can be made in prints and textures or trimmed with decorative tape. For windows not of standard sizes, they may have to be custom-made.

Wood shutters look charming in Early American and other informal interiors, when stained to blend with furniture. They also look fresh when painted or antiqued either to match or contrast with surrounding wall areas.

Window shades run the gamut from translucent cloths that admit a great deal of light to the opaque fabrics that completely darken a room. Room-darkeners are fine for bedrooms, while the others filter glare and lend privacy in rooms used by day. Choose anything from conventional plain white shades to textures, stripes, prints, puckered, nubbed, and embroidered types. Window shade shops will laminate your fabric onto a washable, vinyl-coated window shade. Or, if you are handy, you can do it yourself with the easy, new shade laminating kits that are on the market. Simpler yet, create your very own custom touches on a ready-made window shade with appliqués and other trimmings.

Similar to window shades are matchstick or bamboo blinds that roll up and down, admitting some light through their narrow slits.

Curtains and Draperies

For combining daytime light and evening privacy, opaque draperies on a traverse rod are decorative and functional. Where the view is not desirable or more seclusion is necessary, two fabrics may be best—a semisheer curtain combined with draw draperies. Two or more tiers of café curtains may be used for double function —the top tier remains open to admit light while the bottom tier keeps passersby from seeing in.

To make unattractive windows less noticeable, cover them to match the walls. If you have a patterned wallpaper, for instance, a simple curtain or window shade in matching fabric will give the illusion you want of having the window blend into the background.

If you want windows to be a standout, choose a fabric or color that contrasts with the walls. As an added attention getter, "frame" the window as you would a picture by using either a cornice or a shadow box.

When the shape of a window seems wrong, by all means change it. Instead of placing curtains just on the window, extend them out on the wall to make a small window look wider. If the window is too short, raise the curtains to desired height, using a window shade to conceal the wall area. Valances are also useful in adding inches and hiding unattractive moldings or pipes.

Window Budget Balancers

For ideas about getting a big effect on a small budget, go through the notions and trimmings plus yard goods departments of your favorite store. You'll find many ideas for making inexpensive curtains with a custom look. Among these are kits for making perfect pinch pleats, clip-on hardware that eliminates the need for sewing rings to café curtains, and iron-on appliqués for trimming plain curtains and window shades.

In addition to making curtains and shades from bedsheets, already discussed in the chapter on budget decorating, there are inexpensive fabrics like burlap, sailcloth, cotton, and synthetics. Be sure to consider the texture as well as width of fabric in judging the cost. Sheers may seem inexpensive, but you need at least three times the width of the window for enough fullness to look good. More substantial fabrics drape nicely when made up double the width of the window.

When you own a house or expect to stay in the same apartment for several years, an initial investment in shutters to be filled in with your own fabric panels will prove economical in the long run. Changing the fabric inserts requires only a small financial outlay and the sewing of a few seams, enabling frequent changes that involve a minimum of cost and effort.

Equally versatile is the lambrequin—a boxlike frame of wood built around the top and sides of a window. Paint it, paper it, or cover with fabric to change the look of a room.

It's also refreshing to dispense with conventional treatments altogether and decorate the entire space with rows of colored glassware or plants. Rows of potted plants on shelves or the sill can be used with plants suspended at varying heights from the top of the window or from the ceiling—a great way to lend a fresh, outdoor garden effect to a viewless or ordinary window.

Decorative Accessories

Accessories are the accents that personalize a home. Surround yourselves with meaningful objects related to the things you love or reflecting your taste in design.

The test of whether an accessory adds or distracts is simple. If it contributes anything at all to the total look of a room — color, pattern, or shape — then taking it away would leave something lacking. If you can remove a figurine from the shelf or a bowl of flowers from the table without missing it, then it doesn't belong there.

Strive for variety and individuality. This includes your own handicraft and artwork, family heirlooms, special wedding presents, hobby collections, plus whatever you have gleaned from travel or found as close to home as the neighborhood shops. Some of these ideas may fit in with your plans.

Old books contain wonderful lithographs and drawings that can be photostated at local blueprint houses, mounted on Masonite, and hung on the wall.

Use wicker baskets on the wall, either all in a row or in a free arrangement. Place containers inside the baskets and fill with fern, philodendron, or other indoor plants.

Be a candlestick collector. Pick a type — brass, for example — and collect them in odd sizes, then cluster several at one end of a cocktail table or a skirted round table.

Suspend some of your accessories. Hanging baskets of flowers, plants, or mobiles animate the space around them.

Hang handwoven tapestries, blankets, and rugs on the wall. These can be your own, an heirloom, or something purchased in

the marvelous craft shops of American Indians, East Indians, Mexicans, and any foreign countries you have visited.

Start a collection of varied wooden boxes or woven baskets and use them for storing small objects.

Pick flowers, plants, weeds, and shells, in the woods or at the seashore, and use them for seasonal changes of accessories. Autumn leaves, pumpkins, gourds, pussy willows, and cattails can be combined into lovely centerpieces and other arrangements.

For sentiment as well as beauty, use wedding gifts imaginatively. Try red roses in an ice bucket, dried flowers in a crystal bowl, or a shell collection—memento from your honeymoon—in an oversize brandy snifter.

The Importance of Plants

As living accessories that grow inside your home, plants are in a class by themselves as decorative touches. Even if you are an amateur at gardening, it is possible to maintain vigorous and healthy plants indoors by following the advice of the person who sells them on watering, exposure to light, and other simple tips on care. There are many good books available on caring for plants and using them attractively.

Large plants may be placed on the floor for accent or to make a sparsely furnished room look completed. Use them in hallways or alongside doors, fireplaces, stairs, and picture windows.

Medium-size plants are at home on wall shelves, benches, windowsills, and tables, or in room dividers, hanging baskets, or window boxes.

Small plants are appropriate in planters or dish gardens or on narrow shelves made especially for that purpose.

To get the most out of plants, choose the species that go best with your type of decorating scheme. Large foliage plants go well in a contemporary setting. Among these are many varieties of philodendron, Norfolk island pine, podocarpus, dracaena, schefflera, and dieffenbachia.

Victorian furniture calls for potted palms, rubber plants, and ferns, especially the Boston fern.

In a French Provincial, Louis XV, Georgian, English, or French Regency setting, select smaller plants to blend with the more delicate scale of the furniture. Flowering plants—white or pink azaleas, geraniums, kalanchoes, and small chrysanthemums—are excellent. So are the smaller foliage plants, including ivy and sprengeri. Floor plants should be in the more delicate of large-foliage varieties, like dracaena and cypress. Bonsai, succulents, and snake plants also fit in.

Plant containers, too, must be geared to the theme of the room. Clay pots, which have the advantage of providing healthy growing conditions, look well in most settings, but some period furniture is best complemented by decorative jardinieres. In the latter case, you can always double pot plants by slipping clay pots into an outer container and packing the space with vermiculite or sphagnum moss.

Lighting Your Way

Aside from being necessary, lighting can enhance everything about your home, making rooms seem larger, colors richer, and the atmosphere warmer and cozier.

Don't skimp on lighting. After you have drawn up floor plans for each room, analyze your requirements room by room.

Living rooms. About five portable lamps are necessary in the average living room. A three-light lamp at each furniture grouping provides light for typical home activities. You may want some concealed lighting behind a cornice or valance for a soft, flattering effect that is easy on the eyes. Valance lighting is good for television viewing—it won't reflect on the screen. If you have a card or game table, try a suspended ceiling fixture over it.

Dining rooms. A ceiling fixture, centered over the table and adjustable in height and position, offers the most desirable conditions for dining. Have a dimmer switch put in for creating various moods. Combine this fixture with wall lighting to brighten the whole area.

Bedrooms. A close-to-the-ceiling fixture gives convenient all-over lighting. For reading in bed, night table lamps are fine, but a wall bracket over the bed provides even light across the bed. A bracket on each side of the bed allows one person to read while the other sleeps. Try two portable lamps on the dresser for good grooming. If you have a desk, of course, you will need a lamp there.

Kitchens. Good lighting helps avoid fatigue while working. You should have either a large central fixture, fluorescent wall brackets, or indirect ceiling units. In addition, specific work areas —sinks, ranges, and counters—should be well lit.

Bathrooms. Three fixtures are necessary in most bathrooms to take care of shaving and applying cosmetics. Shielded fluorescent tubes on each side of the mirror will light both sides of the face. To complete the picture, install a ceiling fixture above the wash basin to light the top of the head and reflect under the chin.

When selecting table lamps for reading, be sure they are the correct height. The bottom edge of the shade should be at eye level with the reader. Sit in a chair or sofa and measure the distance from eye level to table top, then take a tape measure when you shop.

Chapter 8
Selecting Your Tableware

If there is one wedding tradition apt to endure forever, it's the centuries-old custom of presenting fine tableware to the bride. What could be nicer than the prospect of receiving gifts that are beautiful, useful, and of lasting value?

The earlier you make your pattern selections and register them with the bridal gift registry consultant at the store you've chosen, the better chance you'll have of acquiring enough place settings to use when you are settled in your new home.

There are many different types of tableware available at all price levels. In flatware and holloware, there is sterling, silver plate, pewter, stainless, chrome, and other metal compositions. What we loosely refer to as china may be "the real thing" or some of its very creditable derivatives like earthenware, ironstone, stoneware, and other ceramics. Glassware may be fine crystal or pressed glass with a high lead content and beautifully cut.

Your own personal preferences and life-style, along with due consideration of how much you can afford to spend or can reasonably anticipate receiving as gifts, will determine what you ultimately decide to start collecting. Couples who hope to attain complete sets of sterling, fine china, and crystal will probably want second sets of less expensive ware for everyday use. If you are choosing from a lower price category with thoughts of acquiring finer items later on, don't think that you have to sacrifice quality or design. There's so much available.

Sterling Silver

Like gold, diamonds, and other precious natural commodities, sterling silver has a practical as well as a romantic side. For years, it has been growing in value faster than money in the bank can draw interest.

Under federal law, an object imprinted with a sterling mark is required to contain 92.5 percent pure silver, with some copper added to harden and increase its wearing qualities. Sterling comes in two finishes—a bright high polish that is most often used, and a softer sheen known as a butler finish. Terms you will hear that pertain to the beauty of silver are: oxidizing, which means the darkening process applied to the design to give rich contrasts; and patina, or the interesting surface silver gradually acquires after being used.

Although much of the value of sterling is intrinsic in the metal itself, design and workmanship are also important and are reflected in the price. The heavier the piece, naturally, the more silver it contains and the more it costs. But also check the feel and balance of each piece in your hand as though you were actually using it. Be sure the shanks are strong and the fork tines smooth.

Rely on familiar brand names to be sure you are getting the best. Generally, similar types of patterns will be in the same price range, and plain is less costly than fancy.

Silver Plate

Similar in appearance to sterling but without its lasting qualities, silver plate is made by coating a base metal, usually a nickel alloy, with pure silver by the process of electroplating. The base metal may be thinly or thickly coated with silver, depending on how long the piece is submerged in the silver and how often the process is repeated. The thicker the coating, the longer the wear. Silver-plated flatware may last anywhere from many years to a lifetime, and can vary greatly in price.

Today better qualities of silver plate are reinforced with an extra coating of silver at points of greatest wear (stress points). Ask about this when you buy, since it is very important to the life of your silver. Other guides to quality are fine design, smooth edges, good balance, and an even application of the silver.

Pick Your Pattern from the Classics

Every art form has its classics, old and new, and silversmithing is no exception. Working with a precious metal that has long been a symbol of value, silversmiths of every generation have created objects of everlasting satisfaction. If you question your ability to pick a sterling pattern today that will look more beautiful than ever on your silver wedding anniversary, read on. Ranging from utterly simple to lavishly decorated, there is one overriding principle—

Flatware

A GUIDE TO PLACE SETTINGS AND SERVING PIECES

THE PLACE SETTING

Place Fork
—the standard, for all meals; for fish course in formal dinner. (Dinner fork slightly larger, available in some patterns.)

Place Knife
—for all but formal meals. (Dinner knife slightly larger than place size, available in some patterns.)

Teaspoon
—perfect for fruits, desserts, fruit cocktails, coffee, tea.

Individual Salad or Pastry Fork
—salad, fish, pies, pastries.

Place Spoon
—for soup, cereal, dessert, and for use as a small serving piece.

Spreader
—or Individual Butter Knife (Hollow or Flat Handle), for butter, on the sandwich tray, for cheeses, relishes, for hors d'oeuvres, on cheese trays.

Cream Soup Spoon
—soup in dishes or bowls, for serving sauces.

Dinner Knife and Fork
—essential for the formal dinner and whenever more than one knife and fork are needed. The size of pieces is scaled larger than place knife and fork. Some may prefer eight-piece place settings since for-

mal entertaining demands the larger knife and fork.

SERVING PIECES

Cream or Sauce Ladle
—ladles gravy, stews, liquid dishes, and dressings, along with cream sauces.

Cold Meat or Buffet Fork
—serves cold meats, chops, and food served on toast, or a variety of platter salads.

Table or Serving Spoon
—serves salads, vegetables, berries, fruits, and desserts.

Pierced Table or Serving Spoon
—for vegetables or fruits served in their juices.

Gravy Ladle
—serves sauces, gravies, or dressings from either boat-shape dishes or round bowls.

Salad-Bowl Servers
—with wooden ends, for graceful, efficient service of tossed salad. (Note: the Cold Meat Fork and the Salad Spoon make a small salad set.)

Tomato or Flat Server
—can be used for tomatoes, cucumbers, eggs, asparagus on toast, or for platter salads.

Sugar Spoon
—for the sugar bowl and for small bowls of mayonnaise or sauce.

Butter Serving Knife
—for use on the butter plate in informal dining and on the cheese tray; for serving paté or individual fish knife.

Olive or Pickle Fork
—in addition to serving olives and pickles, it doubles as a lemon fork and butter pick.

Pie or Cake Knife
—essential for cutting and serving pies and cakes, and for aspics and frozen desserts.

Relish or Jam Spoon
—for relishes, jams, jellies, preserves, and useful as a spoon for serving mayonnaise.

Cheese Knife
—serves brick cheese, and cheese or similar spreads, and can be used for molded jellies.

Cake Breaker
—for layer cakes that tear and crumble under a knife; makes serving easier.

Sugar Tongs
—for use in the sugar bowl or on the candy dish.

Jelly Server
—serves cream cheese, preserves, jams, relishes, jellies, and marmalades.

Bonbon or Nut Spoon
—for nuts, candies, and some canapés.

Lemon Fork
—serves lemon slices.

CARVING PIECES

Slicer
—sharp and slim and long, essential for thin-slicing roasts.

Roast Carving Knife
—for large roasts, fowl, and ham.

Roast Carving Fork
—to hold roasts and fowl skillfully.

Steak Carving Knife
—for steaks and small roasts, fowl, and other meats such as sliced ham.

Steak Carving Fork
—for use with either Carving Knife as a server when roasts or fowl have been sliced or carved.

OTHER INDIVIDUAL PIECES

Cocktail or Oyster Fork
—seafood cocktail, fruit cocktail, lobster.

Coffee or Cocktail Spoon
—after-dinner coffee, baby's feeding spoon, blender for Old-Fashioneds.

Iced Beverage Spoon
—iced coffee, iced tea, fruit drinks, milk shakes, highball mixer, and parfait.

Demitasse Spoon
—for coffee; can be used for condiments, even for salt.

an adherence to good design. A classic is free of momentary fads and true to the age-old philosophy that a man-made object should be perfectly proportioned and expertly crafted. If there is applied decoration, it flows naturally from the shape of the object and usually is inspired by classic motifs, some of them from ancient civilizations. But when you think classic, don't "date" yourself, and try not to work within the confines of labels, like Early American or Louis XV. Classic patterns blend with many styles and periods. To find the type of pattern best suited to you, take your pick from the design categories listed. Let your emotions be your guide in deciding which styles appeal, then consider the decorating plan you have in mind.

ENGLISH 18TH CENTURY

For English silversmiths, as well as cabinetmakers, the eighteenth century was a time of glory that never has been surpassed. No wonder so many of the patterns we love today are reproductions from this era of good design that brought us the furniture styles of Queen Anne, Chippendale, Sheraton, Hepplewhite, and Adam. One pattern typical of the middle part of the century, when carving and curves decorated the chairs and cabinets of Chippendale and others, has V-shape fluting on the fork and spoon, ending in a gentle roll. It is similar to the carving applied to corners of some Chippendale chair backs. There is a feeling of a beautifully proportioned architectural column to the shape of the fork and spoon handles, while the knife curves in a pistol shape. Faithful to the period, the fork has but three tines, while most later forks have four tines. Toward the end of this century there was a return to classic simplicity—the fiddleback is an excellent example. Although elegant in itself, the fiddleback was also used with the shell motif and other applied decoration. In later years, the Americans were to imprint their fiddleback interpretations with eagles or stars. Many brides find this lovely pattern exactly right if they are looking for sterling that lends itself well to monograms. The third in this group of representative English eighteenth-century patterns completes a picture of great design versatility. There is a restrained amount of ornamentation. The scallop shell at the top of the handle provides a rococo touch. The pattern is called the kings pattern and several silver manufacturers have an example in their line. If you long for the elegant yet comfortable atmosphere of English traditional interiors, any one of this distinguished eighteenth-century trio is well worth considering. But because they are all prime examples of pure classic design, they also lend themselves to other interior decorating schemes—American Colonial, French, or even some contemporary settings are very fitting companions for English-inspired sterling.

EARLY AMERICAN

The colonists began making their own silver in about 1630. Like other artisans who looked to England for inspiration, silversmiths used the finest English silver imports as models. There was a considerable time lag, with the Americans still turning out Georgian-style silver well into the nineteenth century, when the English had gone on to their Regency period. To suit the more modest life-style in America, many designs were simplified. A typical pattern has gracefully tapered handles that are ever so delicately fluted with a twisted wire outline of silver.

FRENCH

Decoratively speaking, wonderful things began to happen in France after Louis XV inherited the throne in 1723. Court furniture became smaller in scale, and its curved lines and rococo decoration appealed to the populace. Craftsmen, including silversmiths, set to work in earnest to produce Louis XV designs suitable for just plain folks. The curvilinear feeling of mid-eighteenth-century French design can have scrolls entwined with rosettes repeated from the motifs found on Louis XV chairs. Because they have just enough decoration for those whose taste is neither plain nor fancy, but in between, provincial patterns are ever popular.

ROCOCO

Derived in France in the early eighteenth century, the rococo style might be for you if you admire intricate, skillfully executed designs. From the word *rocaille*, referring to rock and shell gardens, the style uses shells, flowers, and C-scrolls, intertwined in asymmetrical fashion. Pierced work was used on much rococo silver. It has the delicacy of a richly patterned bridal lace.

BAROQUE

The style with a sculptured look, baroque is a natural medium for the silversmith, enabling him to achieve both the weighty, opulent feeling that is so impressive and the graceful contour that gives flatware aesthetic balance. Of seventeenth-century origin, baroque had wide influence in Europe, resulting in much furniture that was overscaled and overly decorated. In silver, however, baroque is at its best. The sculptural quality of this style permits the play of light and shadow, and there is usually some piercing or openwork to sidestep heaviness.

MEDITERRANEAN

By the late fifteenth century, Spanish silversmiths were doing very intricate and finely detailed work. In turn, architects began to copy these patterns for the embellishment of their building exteriors, and furniture makers applied fancy metal work to their designs. This entire period, lasting until about the mid-sixteenth century, became known as Plateresco, derived from the word *platero*, which is Spanish for silversmith. Today, the enthusiasm for all things Mediterranean has led to a revival of small-scaled and very intricately detailed Spanish patterns—a study in black and silver alternating between floral and scroll motifs.

DANISH

Those wonderful people who brought you Hans Christian Andersen now are responsible for proving that modern design can be as heartwarming and romantic as a fairy tale. Young America has been as quick to fall in love with Danish-style flatware as we were to adopt Scandinavian furniture, for both are based on pure, simple lines with a sculptured quality. Decoration is added sparingly only when it enhances the overall shape. The simple motif used on some patterns reflects an updated form of the scrollwork on traditional design.

NEOCLASSIC

It happens every now and then. The ancient, pure classic designs are revived to make history all over again, usually after a wildly extravagant time during which artistic standards break down and a reaction sets in. Throughout Europe in the eighteenth century, an important revival of the Greek and Roman classic art and architecture was touched off by the discovery in 1753 of the Pompeian ruins. The Adam brothers, English architects and furniture designers, led the way back to purity of line, beautifully balanced proportions, and the use of classic motifs—swags, flowers, leaves, masks, and urns. Typical sterling design of the Adam period shows twin garlands clasping the rose.

ROMANTIC

In direct contrast to the classic periods of history, the romantic interludes are eras when flights of fancy take the place of strict adherence to the traditional forms. Associated more with the French and Italian joie de vivre and sentimentality than the American penchant for practicality or the British sense of restraint in design, the romantic school, nonetheless, has universal appeal. Because there is so much romantic tradition attached to sterling, the metal that has for so long been the mainstay of the bridal dowry or trousseau, many brides will settle for nothing less than a flatware pattern that is frankly romantic in feeling. Much decoration is the distinguishing characteristic of this style, including embossing, engraving, and a great deal of repoussé work. The repoussé technique—a method of applying ornamentation to gold, silver, copper, and other metals by hammering it into shape from the underside—has been in use since antiquity. The resultant design, raised in bold relief, has a rich, deep-dimensioned look that captures the play of light and shadow.

CONTEMPORARY

Along with Parsons tables, Plexiglas cubes, built-in storage walls, and the simplest kind of foam seating, unornamented sterling patterns are contemporary classics. They belong to the young at heart who have a bold sense of the dramatic in furnishing a home. The total absence of ornament on all basic items, such as furniture and flatware, offers a marvelous jumping-off place for high-styled, fast-paced, individualized living. Looking more like a product of the sculptor's chisel than the drawing board, a perfectly plain pattern might inspire bold color schemes and offbeat table accessories, yet it would be equally suitable in a conventional, more formal setting.

Monogrammed Silver

Because silver is so rich in tradition and sentiment, many couples like to add the very personal touch of a monogram. The type of monogram that is appropriate depends on the pattern itself. A single letter—your married name or maiden name initial—may be best if the pattern is ornate. If you prefer three initials, these variations are correct: M E S for Mary Ellen Smith, bride of John Doe; M S D for Mary Smith Doe; or an M and J with a D centered underneath for Mary and John Doe.

Letters are either in the same size, or one large and two smaller letters. In the latter case, the large initial is in the middle and generally stands for the surname—small M, large D, small S in that order reads Mary Smith Doe.

Pewter

You can look like long-time collectors with an array of pewter in your home. As early as 1635, there is record of a pewter shop in Salem, Massachusetts. A little over one hundred years ago pewter was evident in almost all American households. Nearly every vessel or utensil, with the exception of knives and forks, was made of pewter. Today, pewter-handled flatware with stainless steel tines, bowls, and blades is also popular. Current shapes, as well as those of Colonial times, are patterned after European design. The covered tankard in seventeenth-century England and America was considered the aristocrat among drinking vessels. Presently, tankards, mugs, porringers, and plates are highly sought after by collectors. With reproductions of early styles, pewter can grace your table and your shelves.

Stainless Steel

The two magic numbers that are important when you buy stainless steel are 18 percent chromium alloy and 8 percent nickel: this special combination of numbers produces a product of outstanding quality. Fine stainless is thickest at points of stress. It's available in a wide array of design styles, in either bright or satin finish.

Couples who are considering stainless steel flatware, whether for a second set or the one and only, will find that patterns are becoming increasingly varied. There is a wide selection of designs in both traditional and contemporary patterns. It also comes in combinations with stoneware or plastic handles.

Since grades of stainless steel range from poor to excellent, look carefully for evidence of quality. Check rims of spoon bowls and tips of fork tines for smoothness and be sure that all surfaces are free of pit marks. Because of its great strength, stainless steel flatware need not be as heavy as silver, but lightweight pieces that look and feel tinny will bend out of shape, whereas the weightier pieces are literally as strong as steel. Aside from strength, look for quality of workmanship and good design. Backs should be finished with the same care as fronts. As in silver, there is a choice of two finishes—a mirror effect and a satin finish. Do remember to be sure that your choice is 18/8.

Holloware

Holloware, as opposed to flatware, is just what the word implies— tableware that is hollow inside, such as a coffee pot or bowl. You may choose holloware in sterling, silver plate, pewter, stainless steel, and other metals.

Silver plate is extremely popular because it goes well with sterling flatware and is much less costly than sterling. For serving and entertaining, a touch of silver is a touch of luxury in items like platters, vegetable dishes, pitchers, ice buckets, tea and coffee services, and candelabra. Many of these pieces are beautifully decorative and should be displayed.

When buying holloware, workmanship and quality are important. Check for smooth, evenly rounded edges, balance, and substantial nontilt bases. Sterling holloware, of course, has all of these features and is seldom purchased in other than quality stores. Plated silver, on the other hand, is available everywhere from the prestige store in your city to the souvenir shop that may be going out of business. Since a well-made, heavily coated piece of silver holloware that will last a lifetime may look pretty much the same as a thinly plated version, purchasing silver-plated holloware at fine stores and looking for brand names associated with the best in silver is a must.

In addition to sterling and silver plate, there are holloware items for your table in stainless steel, pewter, and other metals. The guidelines for buying stainless steel are the same for those already applied to stainless steel flatware—if the piece you are considering is heavy as opposed to tinny, well-designed, and of good quality workmanship, it is worthwhile.

Choosing Your China

The word "china" in current usage includes all categories of dinnerware, but only porcelain or bone china should be defined by that term. There is also stoneware, earthenware, pottery, ceramic glass, plastic, and metal. The qualities of each vary greatly.

CHINA OR PORCELAIN

For beauty, strength, and enduring value, the best quality dinnerware is china. To make bone china, animal bone is mixed with refined clay, feldspar, and quartz. The resultant product has a more bluish appearance than that not containing bone.

Despite its fragile appearance, genuine china is tougher and more resistant to chipping and breaking than other ceramics. The glaze will not crackle, and, even if it does chip, its nonporous body will not absorb food stains.

When shopping, you will naturally be influenced most by pattern and colors, but keep these points in mind.

1. Hold a plate in front of the light. Can you see your hand through it?

2. Balance a plate on three fingers and tap with a pencil. Does it ring with a bell-like tone?

3. Run a finger around the rim or foot of the plate. Is it smooth? Generally it is not glazed. In order to prevent the plate from sticking to the support in firing, the foot is left unglazed, which in no way impairs the quality.

4. Examine the cup handle. Make certain that it is fastened straight on the vertical.

5. Test the rim of the cup. Is it perfectly smooth, without rough or wavy spots?

6. Examine the saucer. Is the depression designed to hold the cup safely and securely?

So much for quality. Part of the price of china, however, is also inherent in the pattern and colors. Certain patterns with deep or vibrant colors bear high price tags. That's because in manufacturing the finest china, colors and glaze coats are fired separately, and the selection of colors that may be used is unlimited. In less expensive varieties, colors and glaze coats are applied first and then fired together. This limits the color selection, since certain colors break down under the intense heat required for glazing.

WHAT YOU'LL NEED

Most brides like to have a minimum of eight place settings of the five basic pieces: dinner plate, dessert/salad plate, bread and butter plate, cup and saucer. Covered vegetable dish, platters, gravy boat, and a tea or coffee set are nice extras that add beauty and elegance to a table setting. Most patterns are kept in open stock for years so you can gradually complete your set.

OTHER DINNERWARE

Alternatives to genuine china, some of them nice enough for entertaining and others intended as second sets for everyday use, are these.

Earthenware. Made of porous baked clay, this is a type of pottery made waterproof by a glazed surface. In its finer forms, earthenware closely resembles china. The clay is less refined and fired at a lower temperature, resulting in a softer ware that is not as durable as china but stronger than pottery. Crazing and discoloration can be caused by extremes in temperature, and chipping is far more frequent than in china.

Stoneware. This is an opaque, clay-colored (grey or brown) pottery. It is high fired and nonporous. The glazes are varied for different effects. Stoneware is finer grained and harder than earthenware, and more durable. Some stoneware can go from oven to table to freezer. Check for manufacturers instructions. Never put plates directly from oven into freezer.

Ironstone. A hard, white stoneware pottery, ironstone was developed in England in the nineteenth century. Most of today's versions have greater thermal properties and strength.

Metal alloys. Practical as well as novel, metal dinnerware can be either pewter or other metal compositions that have the look and feel of genuine pewter. It has the practical advantages of not breaking or chipping and also keeps hot foods hot and cold food and beverages cold. Metal dinnerware is now available in a variety of styles, with emphasis on traditional design.

Molded plastic. Plastic dinnerware is popular for casual dining. It is virtually unbreakable, can be placed in the dishwasher without deterioration, and is resistant to cracking and chipping. You must be careful not to place it in the oven or expose it to open flame. Quality varies considerably, depending on weight and the care used in finishing. Some of the better lines offer such advantages as stain-resistant cups.

Types of Glassware

One of the most ancient artistic materials known to man is glass — a mixture of silica sand, lime, and other substances heated to a fluid state, then blown, pressed, or drawn to obtain the desired shape. Blown glass can be made by hand — meaning someone actually breathes air into it — or by machine, in which the liquid is shaped by compressed air. Pressed glass is put in a mold and forced into shape by a plunger. Drawing is the process of wrapping the molten glass around a core that is later removed.

While these are the basic methods and materials, glassmakers employ so many variations that a lifetime could be devoted to the study of their art. By changing the mixture of raw materials, the shapes, and the means of applying decoration, creators of fine glassware have kept this ancient craft constantly new, exciting, and fascinating to follow.

When glass is made from a mixture that contains a substantial amount of lead, the resultant product is called crystal. Lead imparts a clear, brilliant sparkle. Crystal can be pressed or drawn as well as blown—the ingredients, not the method of manufacture, are the determining factor. The word crystal is also used to distinguish between glass that is clear as opposed to glass that is tinted in various colors, so that a salesperson may describe a certain pattern as available in red, blue, amethyst, and crystal.

START WITH THE BASICS

You will no doubt want to own fine stemware, plus additional less expensive glasses to go with your casual dinnerware. Glasses may be purchased in complete sets of one item—eight goblets, for example—or in place settings.

For a minimum basic place setting, you might want to have the goblet, wine, and sherbet/champagne. Double old-fashioneds and highball glasses are sizes used as barware. But if space is truly a problem, consider the all-purpose goblet. Classically shaped as a bubble or tulip, it looks elegant with milk, tomato juice, or an on-the-rocks drink.

LOOK FOR QUALITY

Much of our fine stemware is blown crystal—thin, clear, and elegant in appearance—and it is usually blown by hand. To be sure you are getting the best, look for these signs of quality:

Examine the shape. There should be a pleasing symmetry between bowl and stem. Ornamentation, if any, should be subtle —the glass itself and the beauty of its shape must not be overshadowed.

Look for clarity, luster. Good glass sparkles. You will find tiny bubbles in any glass, but in fine crystal these are relatively few.

Check the edges for smoothness. Run your finger along bowl and base. Inferior glass may have scratches, beads, or irregularities.

Listen to the ring. Blown crystal resounds with a clear, bell-like tone when tapped with a pencil.

Many lovely stemware patterns are made of pressed glass, the best of which are done by hand. Pressed glass, too, should have a balanced shape, luster, and smoothness. In addition, inspect the finish to be sure there are no prominent mold marks or ridges— these are removed from better glassware by reheating after the mold has been removed. Test the weight of the glass. It should feel strong and substantial.

EVERYDAY GLASSWARE

For everyday use, as well as entertaining at parties where guests will be moving around rather than seated at the dining table, complete sets of inexpensive glassware are a must. Tall tumblers for serving drinks with ice, a set of "on-the-rocks" glasses, plus cocktail and wine stemware should cover average needs.

How to Coordinate China, Glass, and Silver

Selecting tableware is very much like decorating a living room or bedroom. China, glass, and flatware are the "furnishings" that have to live side by side, and the tablecloth is equivalent to the background of a room. You also have to think about color coordination and the degree of formality or informality you want.

The best way to make up your mind about china, glass, and flatware patterns is by looking at them together. Start by looking at the table setting photographs in magazines, then cutting out advertisements for various wares and arranging them together. Once you have an idea of what styles you prefer, head for the stores and ask the salesperson to arrange some actual place settings for you, or to offer suggestions on patterns that she thinks look well together.

Since so many tableware patterns are classics, representing either designs good enough to have survived from the past or the best work of contemporary designers, finding something really lovely in each of the "big three"—china, glass, and flatware—should be no problem. Remember, it's truly personal preference.

When looking at your choices together, observe their effect upon each other. Unless you prefer a very elaborate, formal look, strive for balance between the ornate and the simple. Two patterned and one plain, or two plain and one patterned, is a good rule. Consider, too, what kind of linens and accessories you might be using. To avoid a too-busy overall effect, keep in mind that centerpieces and interestingly textured or patterned cloths are added attention-getters. Pick colorful linens to complement highly decorated china. The more colors in your china pattern, the more color variety you have. White is basic and an easy background on which to mix patterns.

In choosing patterns, look for some kinship between them but not an exact match. Instead of a rose etched on a glass to go with rose-patterned china, consider something plain. Catch the spirit, not the letter, of the design in your silver. Examine the shape and flow of decoration on a plate, then look for a similar feeling in silver or glass patterns.

When You Inherit China or Sterling

If you've been lucky enough to inherit fine tableware, you are off to a good start. The eclectic method of decorating rooms—mixing styles and patterns rather than matching them—makes for interesting table settings, too. Even if your taste runs to contemporary, a lovely old silver or china pattern can be teamed with something new for a change of pace. Take a sample of your heirlooms with you when shopping and see for yourself what the combining possibilities are.

Even when starting out fresh with no family treasures to consider, you may like the idea of using more than one china or silver pattern. Service pieces need not match place settings. The result is often more interesting when your vegetable dishes, tureens, tea and coffee sets, and serving flatware are different but compatible.

Buying Table Linens

Linens are the all-important variables that enable you to achieve many different effects even though you are using the same one or two sets of china, glass, and silver. Your choice of tablecloth is important in determining the degree of formality of the occasion and the colors to be used in centerpieces.

On most formal occasions, white linen damask with napkins to match is the traditional favorite of long standing, with lace or combinations of linen and lace ranking next in popularity. But today anything goes. Fresh seasonal looks of mix and match make table decorating a reflection of your creativity. For correct size, measure the table and allow an equal drop on all four sides of from eight to twelve inches for an informal cloth, fifteen to eighteen inches for the more elegant damasks.

For informal use, the cloth may be of any suitable fabric or color. In linens alone, the variety of weaves is numerous. Bright solids or gay prints in combinations of cotton, linen, and blends are fresh, pretty, and easy to care for. Also, the sky is the limit if you sew your own. So be creative. There is so much selection.

HINTS FOR EVERY DAY

Since most dining for newly married couples is done *à deux*, a creative approach to everyday table settings can add a great deal to the enjoyment of your new home. Aside from setting the table correctly, such niceties as flowers, candles, or hurricane lamps create a warm, intimate mood for an everyday dinner. Change place mats or tablecloths frequently. It gives a lift to weekday meals or weekend breakfasts. With several sets of place mats or cloths that can be cleaned with a damp sponge or put in the washing machine, there is very little effort involved.

AVERAGE LINEN REQUIREMENTS

Many homemakers like to have several tablecloths in both dinner and luncheon sizes, while others find it desirable to make place mats the mainstay of their linen supply. The following represents an adequate supply for daily use and a moderate amount of entertaining.

1. Good dinner cloth with eight or twelve large napkins.
2. Cloths with extralarge napkins (lapkins) for buffets. Another idea—use bright dish towels.
3. Mat sets with matching and contrasting napkins. Remember to mix and match—your look goes further.

How to Set a Table

Once you experience the thrill of owning silver, china, and glassware, you'll want to be sure of using them correctly. It's easy to master the established rules of etiquette because they are nothing more than common sense—everything is put in place for maximum convenience.

The place plate—or service plate, if you are using one—goes in the center, butter plate to the left, and water goblet to the right. If wine is being served, place the wine glass to the right of the goblet. Flatware is then arranged in order of use, starting from the outside. All forks go on the left except the cocktail or oyster fork. Order depends on the course served first. Spoons and knives line up on the right, blades toward plate. The napkin is placed to the left of the forks and may be folded in an oblong, square, or triangle. (Napkins also can be placed on plates or in glasses for alternate looks.) The butter spreader belongs on the butter plate, either across the top or at the right side, but never centered on the plate. Steak knives, when included, are always in addition to place knives and not a substitute for them. Both belong on the table, with the steak knife to the right of the other.

Before the guests sit down, you may have the first course—shrimp cocktail, for example—on the table. Have a saucer under it and set it on the service plate. Leave the service plates on the table for the soup course, then pick them up with the soup bowls or cups and bring in the dinner plates for the main course.

Salad may be served next as a separate course, although some hostesses prefer to combine it with the main course. The Europeans serve salad after a dinner as a "digestif." In serving dessert, you may bring the silver in on the dessert plate after the main course is cleared away, or place it above the center at the beginning of the meal.

THE FORMAL DINNER

Aside from the fact that more pieces generally go into the setting because more courses and wines are served, there are certain variations in custom for formal service. The butter plate and spreader are not used, since butter is not served. The napkin usually goes in the center of the plate and dessert silver is always brought in on the dessert plate. Wine glasses, like flatware, are placed in order of use. A dinner cloth, usually white, is always used, whereas place mats are a popular alternative at informal meals.

BUFFET STYLE

Serving meals buffet style is particularly popular with newlyweds who have many social obligations to repay and often lack the facilities for inviting several guests to a sit-down dinner. There are no set rules for arranging the table except that logic should prevail with artistic effect a close second. Before the guests arrive, do a trial run to be sure you have made it as simple as possible for diners to make their way from one end of the table to the other, first picking up their plates and then helping themselves to whatever they wish. Since food contributes a good deal of color and interest, distribute it rather than bunch it at one end. It's pretty and handy to place flatware for each guest in a napkin and tie with a ribbon or roll it up.

Chapter 9
Time for a Party

Entertaining is an art that people who enjoy friends can usually master with ease. The realm of entertaining is not limited to preparations in the kitchen. Certainly good food and drink touch all the senses and are responded to with delight, but—make no mistake—planning is the keynote to success. Read recipes, plan menus, make shopping lists, discuss wines and beverages. Your efforts will show when your guests arrive, and you won't have to keep scurrying back and forth to the kitchen. In the beginning, do a test run of recipes. This will put you in command of your timing and you can be certain of the results. Experiment with recipes and develop your favorites, then you can build a repertoire. Remember to keep your menu simple and select dishes that can be prepared ahead so that you and your husband will be free to mingle with your guests. If you both can relax and enjoy your own party, everyone else will have fun.

Decide on Type of Party

There are many types of parties that are fun, so consider what time of the day is best suited to your working life. Sunday brunch is an easy time for a first get-together. Friends always will appreciate that one special dish with a salad and scrumptious dessert. Four-course extravaganzas are nice, but certainly not necessary. Can you seat six? If not comfortably, what about a buffet? Buffets are great at any time of day—brunch, a soup/salad supper, wine/cheese party, or cocktail party. The list is endless. Then there is always the possibility, if your apartment is small, of having a sit-down dinner with dessert and coffee as a help-yourself course. It is a perfect way to encourage the guests to circulate.

IT TAKES TWO

Now that there are two of you to give a party as host and hostess, teamwork will cut the work in half. A formula that works well is to have the husband responsible for cocktail hour and clearing away of glasses plus serving wine with dinner, while the wife takes care of the dinner, buffet, or other refreshments. Roles can be reversed when dinner consists of a special dish prepared by the man of the house. Through trial and error, you can evolve a suitable system.

In advance of a party, make up lists of tasks that should be attended to and divide them between the two of you. These are usually necessary:

Make out a budget, deciding how much you can spend for food, beverages, and table decorations.

Check table linens, silver, dishes, serving trays, etc., and have everything clean, polished, and ready.

Arrange to borrow extras such as table and chairs, china and glass, extra coffee maker, etc.

Plan menu or refreshments and make out market lists for day before and day of the party, including last-minute purchases such as flowers.

Check bar supplies and plan to replenish your stock as needed.

If the party is outdoors, be sure the barbecue is in working order and there is plenty of charcoal, gas or whatever fuel is needed.

Make up a schedule for cleaning the house, a little at a time, several days before the party.

Check recipes for dinner or buffet and be sure most steps can be taken before guests arrive. A pot that has to be watched or a sauce that must be made at the last minute detracts from the fun of being a hostess, so if it can't cook by itself or be made in advance except for a few last minute steps, why not change the menu?

Make up two food preparation lists based on the menu, one for steps to be taken before guests arrive and the second to remind you of what needs to be done later. Tape the second list to the kitchen wall or refrigerator. A timer placed where you can hear it ring from the living room is marvelous for enabling you to relax between finishing one task and starting another.

Serving Drinks at Home

The spirited party generally starts with the host offering guests some liquid refreshment. A round of drinks stimulates the flow of conversation at any hour. One way to avoid having the fully equipped bar, is to offer a house drink. For example, a pitcher of margaritas is perfect, if dinner fare is to be Mexican, then beer and wine or sangria is a complement to the meal. Another is to offer wine—both white and red in large decanters. You don't need a fully stocked bar to be good hosts, only your imagination.

WELL-STOCKED BAR

The basics for a well-stocked bar vary with your geographical region—in the south, for example, bourbon is a popular whiskey. In some areas the spirited choice is Scotch. Then you should plan to stock your mixers—ginger ale, tonic water, club soda, bitter lemon—nearby. Ice is a must for mixed drinks and an ice bucket is handy. Other equipment nice to have for a bar are:

Jiggers	Lemon stripper
Knife	Pitcher
Blender (from kitchen)	Bottle opener
Strainer	Corkscrew
Serving tray	Bar spoon
Cocktail napkins	Ice tongs
	Little cutting board

Garnishes for drinks

Lemon	Olives
Lime	Angostura bitters
Orange	Cocktail onions
Maraschino cherries with stems	Superfine sugar

For your basic bar

1 bottle of each:

Scotch	Vodka
Bourbon	Dark rum
Canadian or Irish whiskey	Light rum
Gin	Dry vermouth
Blended whiskey	Sweet vermouth

Fill-ins to complete a bar

Aperitif wine (Dubonnet, Lillet)

Italian bitters (Campari or Punt et Mes)

Dry sherry

Medium dry sherry
Port
Quality cognac
Assorted brandies (after-dinner drinks)

GLASSES

The most basic are: Old-Fashioned glasses 10-12 oz. size. They are available in both single and double sizes and are used for on-the-rocks drinks. Highball glasses are for tall drinks. All-purpose bubble- or tulip-shape wine glasses can be used for any drink. Stemmed glasses keep drinks colder longer and always have that elegant look.

Other glassware that is nice to have includes: sherry or port glasses; brandy snifters (great for desserts, too); beer mugs or pilsners; decanters.

RECIPES FOR BASIC DRINKS

Martini: ½ oz. dry vermouth, 2 oz. gin, vodka, or white rum. This is a 4-to-1 proportion. For a drier martini, proportions can be 5-to-1 or 8-to-1.

Whiskey Sour: 1½ oz. lemon juice, ½ tsp. sugar, 1½ oz. blended whiskey. Variations: substitute Scotch or gold-label rum for blended whiskey.

Manhattan: 1½ oz. blended whiskey, ½ oz. sweet vermouth, dash Angostura bitters. For a Dry Manhattan, substitute dry vermouth for the sweet.

Daiquiri: ½ tsp. sugar, ½ oz. lime juice, 1½ oz. white rum.

Bloody Mary: 1½ oz. vodka or white rum, 3 oz. tomato juice, ½ oz. lemon juice, dash Worcestershire sauce, dash salt, dash pepper, drop of Tabasco.

Screwdriver: 1½ oz. vodka or white rum in orange juice.

WINES

There are vast selections of wines available on the market today and the price range varies. Wine is "The Drink" to accompany your meal in Europe, and Americans are definitely following suit. You don't need to adhere to fast rules of red wine with meat and white for fish or chicken. Yes, there are reasons why, and they are valid, but we Americans tend to like our refreshment cool and chilled white or rosé wines are pleasant drinking.

When it comes to buying wines, seek out a reliable dealer who can answer your questions and whose opinion you can rely on. Be sure you indicate what you are having for dinner. Most wine merchants will tell you about "special" wines that are being featured to enable you to take advantage of a good buy.

Another point when shopping for wines is to learn to read a label. Appellation Controllé in French wines is your guarantee that the wine-making techniques and correctness of type or grapes is authentic. This is a quality control.

Mis en bouteille au chateau means made and bottled at the "Chateau" or estate. *Mis en bouteille* does not mean estate bottled.

WINE CATEGORIES

Table wines. These wines, made from fermented grapes that have been clarified and aged for various periods of time, are served with food.

Fortified wines or dessert wines. These are also fermented, but after fermentation takes place a brandy is added. This adds alcohol content. Fortified wines come in degrees of sweetness. The principal types are: sherry, port, and Madeira. Others in this category are marsala, muscatel, tokay.

Aperitif wines. These generally come from "secret" recipes and are an infusion of wines with herbs, roots, etc. Famous in this group are Vermouth (which comes dry and sweet), Dubonnet (red and white), Lillet, Punt et Mes, Campari, and Byrr. There are many other aperitif wines available.

Sparkling wines. The most famous, of course, is champagne. Then comes a Blanc de Blanc, Asti Spumante, Cold Duck, and Sparkling Burgundy. The German version is called Sekt. Sparkling wines are effervescent and very drinkable ... perfect for every occasion.

Store table wines lying on their side. This keeps corks immersed in wine and, therefore, swollen and airtight. Never place wines near heat or in sunlight. And, certainly, don't let them freeze.

SERVING WINE

If red wine is the choice for your dinner party, remove it from the rack several hours ahead and stand upright. If there is any sediment it will rest on the bottom of the bottle. Remove the cork at least one hour before serving. This allows the wine to "breathe." Breathing allows the air to develop the body bouquet and flavor. Wipe inside neck of the bottle. Red wines should be served at room temperature about 65°F. Once opened, red wines should be stored in refrigerator and removed a few hours before serving.

White wine should be chilled in the refrigerator for a few hours. The ideal temperature for serving should be between 45°–50°F. If the wine is chilled too deeply, you lose some of the flavor.

To reduce the temperature of a white wine more quickly, place in a bucket of ice and water for about twenty minutes.

Fill glasses about one-third full. Tip: to pour wine without drips, turn bottle quickly to the right.

Try to complement foods and wine. A salad and wine just don't mix, as the vinegar taints the taste of the wine. To enrich the flavor of a soup, add a fortified wine, sherry, or Madeira.

GUIDE TO WINE TYPES

RED WINES

France. Clarets from Bordeaux: Medoc, Graves (sometimes white as well), St. Emilion, Pomerol. From the Cote de Rhone: Chateauneuf-du-Pape. From Burgundy: Pinot Noir (a varietal wine made from grape of same name), Beaujolais.

Italy. Chianti, Barolo, Bardolino, Barbera, Grignolino, Valpolicella.

Spain. Rioja.

WHITE WINES

France. From Burgundy: Montrachet, Chablis, Meursault, Pouilly-Fuisse. From Bordeaux-Sauterne (sweet, for dessert only): Graves, Entre-deux-mers. From Loire-Vouvray: Muscadet, Pouilly Firme, Sancerre. From Alsace: Gewurtztraminer, Sylvaner, Pinot Blanc, Riesling, Muscat d'Alsace, Tokay d'Alsace.

Italy. Verdicchio, Orvieto, Soave.

Spain. Rioja.

Portugal. Vinho Verde.

American wines from California are using the names of the variety of grape from which it is produced. The red Pinot Noir is the grape in a Burgundy wine. The grape in a Bordeaux, the Cabernet Sauvignon; for Beaujolais, the Gamay. Zinfandel is unique from California and unknown in Europe. American wines can be marvelous values. Talk with the proprietor of your local wine and liquor shop about his selections and recommendations. Don't hesitate to ask questions and experiment until you find the ones that appeal to your palate.

Some white wines from California also use varietal names — Riesling, Chenin Blanc, Pinot Blanc, Pinot Chardonnay, Sylvaner.

Music Sets the Mood

A nice touch for any party is the right kind of music to establish a particular mood. The kind of cocktail party or buffet supper where everyone makes lively conversation and moves freely about the room benefits from an accompaniment of bright tunes, while the flavor of Italian, French, or Spanish cuisine is enhanced by music of the appropriate country playing softly in the background. Unless you are supplying music for dancing, keep it low enough to avoid interference with conversation.

What's for Dinner?

At sit-down dinners and buffets, you can keep the menu simple yet still treat your guests to something they don't often have that conveys the festive feeling of an evening out.

Giving your dinners and buffet suppers a foreign flavor is one way to make them intriguing. Especially popular are Oriental dishes, many of which can be stir-fried quickly in a wok while guests sit around the kitchen. A wok and ring—a pan with rounded bottom and the circle of metal that holds it in place over the burner—can be purchased inexpensively in housewares departments or gourmet shops and will introduce you to a whole new world of good taste and good nutrition.

Also popular are fondues, which can be served in the living room, with guests dipping bread cubes into a bubbling pot of melted cheese. Dessert fondues are heavenly when you are having guests for coffee and cordials and want something they will think of as special.

For sit-down dinners there is paella, the seafood and chicken specialty of Spain that is as colorful as a fiesta. For other dinner and buffet suggestions, as well as ideas for brunch and lunch, try some of the following.

SHOW-OFF MENUS FOR TWO
Snappy Sunday Fare

Fresh Whole Strawberries	Canadian Bacon
Sautéed Mushrooms on Toast	Coffee Suisse
Scrambled Eggs with Curry	

Versatile eggs! Scramble them with all sorts of pep-ups like ham, herbs, chopped pepper, pimiento, or mozzarella cheese.

To prepare mushrooms: melt 4 tablespoons of butter in a skillet until sizzling. Add 1 pound sliced mushrooms and sauté until lightly browned. Stir and shake pan gently—careful, don't over cook. Season to taste with salt, freshly ground pepper, and a quick dash of Worcestershire sauce. Serve on buttered toast points. Top with chopped fresh chives and parsley. Garnish with crisp bacon. Tip: the strawberries are elegant served in a crystal bowl with cocktail picks. Dip them in champagne.

Beautiful Brunch

Champagne	Sweet Butter
Melon Wedges with Lime	Currant Jelly
Chicken Hash Frittata	Coffee or Tea
Croissants	

Called "brunch," it means any time of the day you would like such tasty fare as our chicken hash, blueberry pancakes and syrup, or waffles with creamed ham.

For chicken hash frittata: sauté 1 small onion and about 2 tablespoons green pepper, both finely chopped, in 2 tablespoons of butter and 1 tablespoon of oil. Cook until just soft and onions are transparent. Add 1½ cups of diced cooked chicken. Mix and season to taste with a little salt, freshly ground pepper, and a sprinkling of tarragon. Add 2 tablespoons each of chopped parsley and slivered almonds. Mix together and press the mixture in skillet; cover and cook for about three minutes, or until heated through. Pour in 2 slightly beaten eggs mixed with 2 tablespoons grated Parmesan cheese and cook on low heat just until set. Slip under broiler until eggs and cheese are lightly browned. Divide and serve immediately.

Luscious Lunch

Wine: Chilled Soave   Italian Rolls
Fettucini Al Burro   Fresh Raspberries Madeira
Artichokes Vinaigrette on Greens   Cappucino

Trust the romantic Romans to come up with delicious Fettucini —great any way you serve it.

To make fettucini: cook 1 package (8 oz.) noodles and toss gently with 1 cup of Parmesan cheese, and ½ cup melted sweet butter. Serve hot with additional grated cheese. Tip: for perfect noodles, avoid overcooking. Six to eight minutes is plenty. To stop noodles cooking, add a cup of cold water to boiling water. Drain quickly. Variation: to make Fettucini Alfredo, prepare noodles as above and add ½ cup warm heavy cream with the butter.

Sumptuous Supper

Wine: Chablis   Steamed Asparagus with
Seafood Crepes   Lemon Butter
    French Vanilla Espagnole

Long, lingering suppers are the excuse for show-off crepe making. Fillings are endless—chicken, ham, cheese, fresh fruits and cream, fresh or canned seafood.

Prepare your favorite cookbook crepe or crepe pan recipe in advance. Crepes can be stored in refrigerator or freezer. To make the filling, flake crabmeat or tuna or cut up cooked shrimp in small pieces. Mix with enough undiluted cream of celery or mushroom soup to hold together. Add a dash of curry powder, freshly chopped parsley, and a little sherry. Salt lightly and add a pinch of white pepper. Put a spoonful on each crepe. Roll up and put in a buttered baking dish. Sprinkle with melted butter and bake in a preheated 350°F. oven until well heated (about 20 minutes). Serve with a curry sauce made by mixing ½ cup of milk and a dash of curry powder with extra soup from the filling mixture. Tip: to make Espagnole sauce for ice cream, mix ½ cup raspberry jam with 2 tablespoons of Madeira wine. Fabulous!

SHOW-OFF DINNERS FOR FOUR

Sunday Night Supper

Wine: Beaujolais	Button Mushrooms and
Boeuf Stroganoff	Cucumbers Marrakech
(Beef in Sour Cream)	Mandarin Oranges
Parslied Noodles	Cointreau
Coffee	

This is a fabulous dish to serve for a buffet or dinner party because you can prepare it almost completely ahead of party time.

To make boeuf Stroganoff, slice 2 pounds of tenderloin or sirloin into slices cut into ½-inch strips (easier to do if you freeze the meat partially). Heat 4 tablespoons of butter in a large skillet and brown the meat well on all sides. Add ½ pound sliced mushrooms, 1 large sliced onion, and 2 tablespoons chopped dill. Cook until onions are soft and liquid is reduced. Add 1 can (10½ oz.) condensed beef broth, ½ cup dry white wine, a sprinkling of salt, and a grind or two of pepper. Cover and simmer for 10 minutes or until meat is fork tender. (If you are making it ahead, cook to this stage.) Stir in sour cream; heat, stirring constantly. Garnish with chopped dill and serve with cooked rice. Tip: for mushrooms and cucumbers Marrakech, add 1 tablespoon prepared mustard and 1 clove garlic, cut in half, to ½ cup oil and vinegar dressing. Drain one 8-ounce can button mushrooms and marinate several hours, preferably overnight. Just before serving, remove garlic and add two unpeeled, thinly sliced cucumbers and 2 tablespoons yogurt. Toss gently and arrange on crisp lettuce.

Dinner For All Seasons

Wine: Chilled White Burgundy

Suprêmes au Vin Blanc
   (Chicken Breasts)

Duchess Potatoes

Bibb Lettuce and
   Tarragon

Peaches Princess

Coffee

Chicken, from fried to fancy, is an economy if you're not filthy rich, but frantically hungry—especially when beautified with white wine.

To prepare suprêmes, skin and bone 4 whole chicken breasts; cut each in half (each half or filet is a suprême); or split breasts and leave bone on, if desired. Dip suprêmes in flour and shake off excess. Melt ⅓ cup butter in a large skillet. Sauté on both sides until golden brown; remove and keep warm. Pour 1 cup of canned chicken broth into skillet and stir over medium heat until all the brown bits are loosened and well blended. (That's what makes the sauce so rich!) Add ½ teaspoon crumbled leaf rosemary, a dash of salt and freshly ground pepper, follow with ½ cup of dry white wine; return chicken breasts to skillet; lower heat; cover and simmer about 5 minutes. Arrange suprêmes on a platter. Top with chopped parsley. Serve the pan juices in a sauceboat. Tip: to degrease can of chicken broth, place in freezer for 10 minutes.

Skim fat from top. Tip: for a delicious dessert, heat canned cling peaches in a mixture of ⅓ cup each of plum preserves, currant jelly, and strawberry jam, spiked with brandy and kirsch to taste. A treat served over vanilla ice cream topped with toasted almonds.

Black Tie Special

Wine: St. Emilion

Grillades New Orleans
  (Fancy Steak)

Herbed Rice Pilaf

Watercress and Endive Salad

Crème-de-Menthe Parfait

Coffee

Dramatize plain beefsteak with an ambrosia of flavorful sauce and a selection of zesty spices.

To prepare grillades, cut a 2-pound, boned sirloin steak into 8 pieces (½ inch thick). Brown quickly on both sides in 3 tablespoons hot oil; remove and keep warm. Add 1 tablespoon flour to the oil in the pan. Stir-scrape quickly until golden brown. Add 1 cup finely chopped onion, 1 clove of minced garlic, 1 green pepper, finely chopped. Cook together until soft. Add 1 can (about 1 lb.) whole, peeled tomatoes, about 2 tablespoons chopped parsley, ½ teaspoon of crumbled leaf thyme. Add a hefty seasoning of freshly ground pepper and a dash of salt. Mix well, add the steak grillades. Cover and simmer over low heat 35 to 40 minutes or until tender. Check occasionally: if the meat sticks to the pan, or if the gravy becomes too thick, add a little boiled water to the pan. Tip: for crème-de-menthe parfait, layer crème de menthe and vanilla ice cream in parfait glasses, top with grated chocolate.

SHOW-OFF BUFFETS FOR SIX OR EIGHT

Oriental Style

Wine: Cabernet Sauvignon

Indonesian Beef Curry

Egg

Coconut

Pilaf of Rice
Green Pepper
Peanuts
Scallions

Endive and Chicory Salad
Flat Bread
Gingered Melon Wedges

Spice up an oriental supper with curry, condiments, and conversation for the supreme show-off entertainment.

To make Indonesian beef curry, brown 4 pounds of boneless round or chuck, cut in 1-inch cubes, in a Dutch oven using about ½ to ¾ cup of fat or oil. Add 3 cups of chopped onion and 4 cloves of mashed garlic, cooking until soft and lightly browned. Mix together 2 teaspoons salt, a few grinds of pepper, 4 tablespoons curry powder, 2 cans (10 oz. each) condensed beef broth, 2 cans (8 oz. each) tomato sauce, and 2 tablespoons lemon juice. Add to the browned beef cubes, cover, and cook over medium heat 1½ hours. Uncover and cook 30 minutes longer or until meat is tender and sauce is reduced. Serve it with rice pilaf garnished with freshly chopped parsley. Curry is super accompanied by chopped pepper, peanuts, coconut, scallions, and egg. Tip: a perfect dessert is melon wedges dusted with a mixture of powdered sugar and ginger.

American Specialty
Wine: Zinfandel
Smoked Virginia Ham Madeira
Glazed Baby Carrots

Bibb Lettuce and Beets
  with French Dressing
Fruited Trifle Creme

A baked, glazed Virginia ham is really delicious accompanied by a Madeira Sauce. Simple, yet special.

To prepare sauce, simmer together one cup of Madeira wine (or a good ruby port), 1 cup of orange juice, ½ cup of dark seedless raisins, ½ cup of red currant jelly, 1 teaspoon dry mustard, and a couple of good dashes of lemon and orange peel along with a sprinkling of allspice. If you want to thicken it, blend about a tablespoon of cornstarch with the orange juice before adding to mixture. Tip: for a glorious ending, layer sliced peaches, halved seedless grapes, sliced dried figs, and whole strawberries in a crystal bowl; then top with cooked, cooled vanilla pudding seasoned with 3 tablespoons sherry wine. Circle the bowl with ladyfingers and wait for the raves!

Mexican Olé

Beer

Party Chili en Casserole

Steamed Rice

Corn Chips

Berry Compote in Rum

Lettuce

Chopped Onion

Avocado and Tomato Slices
    with Garlic Dressing

Make a super pot of chili for a south-of-the-border supper that is self-service, tasty, and stylish.

For chili, brown 1½ pounds of ground round or chuck in a little fat or oil (you don't need much, as the meat has some fat in it). Break up meat with the fork gently as it cooks. Add 1½ to 2 cups of chopped onion and 1 large green pepper, seeded and chopped. Cook until the onions and peppers are soft. Add 2 cans (1 lb. each) whole, peeled tomatoes, 1 bay leaf and salt, ground cloves (just a dash), chili powder (1 to 2 tablespoons), and hot-pepper sauce. Cover and simmer for 2 hours, adding tomato juice if necessary to keep chili from getting too thick. Add 1 can (about 1 lb.) kidney beans after cooking for two hours. Remove the bay leaf. Pour in casserole. Serve with accompaniments arranged so guests can layer plates first with lettuce, then rice, chili, onion, and chips. Tip: for dessert, marinate blueberries, raspberries, and strawberries in a mixture of 3 tablespoons superfine sugar and 1 cup of rum. Serve in your prettiest crystal compote. Everyone will feel refreshed and pampered.

Moroccan Intrigue

Wine: White Rioja	Dipping Sauce Verte
Crudites	(Green Sauce)
(Crispy Vegetables)	Chicken Moroccan
Nutted Rice	Pineapple au Kirsch Ambrosia
Preserved Kumquats	(with Coconut)

Add a spirited theme to your next dinner! Make it Moroccan with the intrigue of spices and herbs from Mediterranean bazaars.

Prepare chicken Moroccan in a Dutch oven. Split 8 whole chicken breasts. Brown breasts in ½ cup oil. Add 2 large sliced onions and 2 mashed garlic cloves, cooking until they are soft. Do not brown. Add about 1 tablespoon salt, 1 teaspoon of crushed chili pepper, 2 teaspoons ground coriander, and ½ teaspoon cumin with 1 cup chicken broth. Simmer all this for 30 minutes, then add 1 cup white raisins soaked in ½ cup of sherry, and 1 cup blanched almonds. Cook for 15 minutes more or until the chicken is tender. Add more chicken broth if you need it. Serve with hot steamed rice garnished with toasted peanuts. Tip: crudites are chilled and crisped vegetables—carrot strips, celery fans, radish roses, and pepper circles. Serve with a Sauce Verte made by blending ½ cup sour cream, ½ cup mayonnaise, and a mixture of 1 tablespoon each of chives, parsley, watercress, 1 teaspoon dried tarragon, and salt and pepper to taste.

End of a Perfect Evening

The finishing touch to any evening is a good, hot cup of freshly brewed coffee or tea. To send your guests home on an upbeat note, learn the few easy steps to perfect tea or coffee every time you plan to serve it.

HOW TO BREW GOOD COFFEE

Here are six guidelines on how to make a delicious cup of coffee, outlined by the Coffee Brewing Center of the Pan-American Coffee Bureau.

Begin with clean equipment. Baking soda neutralizes existing flavors and leaves no trace of its own. Never scrub pot with an abrasive — it leaves scratches and pits that trap oil buildup.

Use best water available. Bottled or distilled water is, of course, ideal. Naturally soft or slightly hard is okay. Water softeners form a gelatinous mass in grounds. Hard water causes a buildup of mineral deposits. Some automatic brewing systems are building in carbon filters to rid water of impurities. For automatic drip systems, start with cold water.

Brew at proper temperature. That temperature is 195°–205°F. — just under boiling. If you're using the drip filter method, pour to half-way up filter, return remaining water to boiling then, when it has dripped through, pour in remainder of water.

Select proper grinder. The finer the grind, the more flavor in extraction. Percolator coffee is best when brewed at regular grind. Water passes coffee over and over. Since water passes through drip only once, use a finer grind. Experiment for the grind that produces the flavor you prefer.

Measure the amount of coffee accurately. Rule of thumb is one part coffee to six parts water. That is, two level tablespoons to a six-ounce measure of water. Strength is your own preference.

Brew coffee proper length of time. Brewing process begins when hot water touches ground coffee. Most electric pots are timed properly. Too long a brewing time extracts bitter flavors.

Do note that coffee has the best flavor upon completion of brewing. Lengthy standing in the pot has a detrimental effect on the quality of the flavor.

METHODS OF BREWING

Drip brewing: here's the current popular method. Electric automatic drips are produced by various manufacturers. The manual or electric methods are essentially the same. Hot water passes through ground coffee just once. Automatic systems are convenient because the machine heats water to proper temperature.

Percolation: previously popular. It is one method of heating water, which passes through a tube, to then spray water over ground coffee. Reasons coffee purists are not fond of this method is that boiling water passes over grounds many times, overextracting, which can produce a bitter taste.

Neapolitan: this coffee pot saves you the step of boiling water and then pouring it over grounds. This upside-down pot boils water in pot—then is removed from heat and flipped over to let it drip through basket into serving pot.

Plunge pot: this is considered the choice of gourmets. Place coffee in carafe then pour in boiled water, stir, then place screened plunger on top. Wait three to five minutes. Filter holds grounds on bottom of pot.

Cold water coffee: in this method, coffee is soaked in cold water to produce a concentrate. Hot water is added to this concentrate to produce an instant cup of coffee.

Espresso: this is a strong, darker roast coffee made by forcing boiling water and steam through fine grounds. There are electric espresso machines, favorites in France and Italy, and also manual methods. Electric machines can be costly and are interesting conversation pieces.

TYPES OF COFFEE BLENDS

Personal taste dictates preference. If something exotic is not available where you live, there are many places to order by mail.

Remember to experiment with blends, roasts, and grinds until you find something you enjoy.

It's fun and easy being a coffee gourmet.

HOW TO MAKE GOOD TEA

There are three different types of tea: black, green, and oolong. All three types come from the same tea bushes cultivated in the same careful way in the same rich tropical lands. What happens after the leaves are picked is what makes them different.

Black tea: this tea undergoes a special processing treatment that turns the leaves black. This gives the tea a rich, hearty flavor — the kind most Americans like best.

Green tea: one of the steps — oxidation — is omitted here. As a result, this tea is green in appearance and has a light color when brewed.

Oolong tea: this is a compromise between black and green tea. It's semiprocessed so its leaves are partly brown and partly green. Oolong tea also has a light color.

FOUR GOLDEN RULES FOR BREWING TEA

The Tea Council of the U.S.A. offers these rules for making a delicious and refreshing cup of tea.

Use your teapot. A teapot is best because it helps keep the water hot during the brewing period.

Use fresh cold tap water. Bring to a full rolling boil. Water that has been reheated in a kettle gives tea a flat taste. Only boiling water poured over the tea produces the full flavor.

Use one teaspoon of tea or one tea bag per six-ounce cup. A tea bag is equivalent to a teaspoon of tea . . . just enough to give you a full-bodied cup of tea.

Brew by the clock — three to five minutes, depending on the strength you like. It takes time for the leaves to unfold and release their flavor. So don't guess—time it by the clock.

HOW TO MAKE REALLY GOOD ICED TEA

Nowadays, when you're hot and thirsty, you automatically think of a glass of iced tea. It's as easy to prepare as hot tea. Follow the four golden rules, but use 50 percent more tea to allow for the melting ice. For example, you'd use four tea bags to make four cups of hot tea. But to make four glasses of iced tea, you would use six tea bags.

Chapter 10
Equipping Your Kitchen

Thanks to modern innovations and inventions that keep getting better all the time, meal preparation is a lot simpler than it used to be—and kitchens are prettier and more colorful. What you need for your own first kitchen depends on the degree of elaborate food preparation you'll be doing, plus space available for storage, and the demands that will be made on your time by activities outside the home.

If both of you are working, and perhaps adding night school to your schedule, chances are you'll adhere to simple menus, sometimes relying on convenience foods for shortcuts. You'll probably find some equipment as useful as an extra pair of hands.

Consider weekends when you'll both have time for gourmet cooking. Equipment for specialties of your home, from paella to Peking duck, can be stored away on a high shelf if not used for everyday items. So if you want a paella pan, Chinese wok, crepe pan or fondue set, don't hesitate to have them.

Later in this chapter you'll find two illustrated lists—the first containing items considered essential for most people, and the second adding extras that are nice to have. Adapt these lists to your own requirements by going over them and deciding which items are necessary for the type of meals you plan to prepare.

When selecting, look for items that are functional and harmonious in color and design. Then keep the items you use most frequently on your counter. Look also for dual-purpose equipment —small appliances and gadgets that do more than one job, and cookware pretty enough to double for serving are best bets.

How to Buy Pots and Pans

Aluminum, stainless steel, copper, and cast iron are the metals most widely used in the manufacture of pots and pans. In addition, oven-to-tableware made of various other materials is becoming increasingly popular. Here are some facts about each.

Aluminum. A durable, lightweight metal, aluminum heats quickly and evenly, with no hot spots to cause burning or sticking of foods to the pan. Therefore, it is a good choice for both baking and top-of-the-stove cooking. If your pots and pans are of fairly heavy gauge aluminum they will resist warping and denting and give years of service. Extra-thick aluminum pots with tight fitting covers give the nutritional advantages of waterless cooking, in which more vitamins and minerals are preserved. Aluminum does become discolored from certain minerals in food and water, particularly where water is hard, but these stains can be removed.

Stainless steel. Pots and pans of stainless steel are more expensive, but practically indestructible, extremely light in weight, and easy to clean. This metal performs best when used to cook foods in water or other liquids. It is less effective for frying because steel can develop hot spots that cause food to brown unevenly. By using steel with another metal—copper or aluminum bottoms—manufacturers have combined the best features of two materials.

Copper. Because this is such an attractive metal, homemakers who plan to display pots and pans invariably choose copper, or stainless steel with copper bottoms. Copper is expensive but extremely durable. It heats evenly and conducts heat faster than other metals. Although it does require special care after each use to retain its beauty, there are cleansers that keep copper bright with little effort. French copper can be lined with tin, which needs special care. American copper pans are sometimes lined with steel for easier inside care.

Cast iron. The slow, even heat provided by cast iron makes this a material gourmet cooks insist upon for certain dishes. Cast iron is heavy and durable, but requires care to retard rust spots. Many cookware lines now feature cast iron coated with colorful enamel finishes that are a bright addition to the kitchen and look attractive for serving at the table.

Ceramics. Porcelain, glass, stoneware, and other materials offer the advantage of being able to cook, serve, and sometimes even freeze food in the same attractive pot. There are colors and designs to match dinnerware patterns. Some cook-and-serve ware may be used for top-of-the-range cooking, while other types are meant to be used only in the less intense heat of the oven. To derive the maximum benefit from owning this kind of cookware, it is important to know what temperature extremes it will withstand. Never place directly in freezer after cooking.

Nonstick finishes. The most famous nonstick finish is probably "Teflon," a registered trademark of DuPont. The solid nontoxic plastic polymer has inherent nonstick, is easy to clean, and dishwasher safe. DuPont has a new nonstick finish called "Silverstone." It is a tougher nonstick finish and fused in a three-layer system to specially prepared cast and rolled aluminum. This finish is used on heavier gauge products. There are other nonstick silicone resins that have many of the above qualities.

Kitchen Cutlery

One of the most important tools of all is the kitchen knife, which is wielded on an average of thirty-two times a day for slicing, paring, trimming, coring, and spreading. Good stainless steel cutlery can last a lifetime if treated with care. Carbon steel requires more care, but holds a better edge. Never use a knife for opening bottles, cutting string, or other purposes for which it was not intended. It blunts the edge. For sharpening, a rough-textured sharpening stone or steel is recommended. These knives will prove most useful in your kitchen:

Paring knives with short blades, 2½″ to 3½″ long, and sharp and tapered points. Use the tapered point for peeling and slicing lemons; the sharp point for preparing salad garnishes and many other uses.

Utility knife with slender blade, 5″ to 7″ long, necessary when the paring knife is too small. Use for halving and trimming fruits and vegetables, boning meats, dicing vegetables.

French knife or chef's knife, with an angled blade 8″ to 10″ long, is perfect for carving hot roasts or mincing onions.

Narrow slicer with a flexible 7″ to 12″ blade is best for slicing bread, serving poultry, or cutting melon rings.

Carving knife with stiff blade, 9″ or longer, for roasts or fowl.

Boning knife, 6″ long, for boning ham, leg of lamb, and other cutting operations.

Light cleaver, 6″ to 7″ long, for cutting joints, lobsters, poultry, and mincing.

Serrated edge bread knife for bread, cakes, and pastries.

Frozen food cutter with deeply serrated edge for cutting while food is still frozen.

The most basic three are: a 3½″ paring knife; an 8″ French chef's knife; and a 12″ slicing knife.

Electrical Appliances

Putting electricity to work is ecological and convenient. Select appliances by starting with those that can save the most time and effort. Certain multipurpose appliances, like the small hand mixer or blender, are definitely worth the space they occupy. Bear in mind that any appliance is more useful when you can keep it handy rather than having to store it where it is hard to reach.

To help you decide, here are some facts about small appliances most popular with newlyweds.

Coffee makers. They shut off automatically when the brew is just right, then keep it hot without reaching the boiling point. You can choose from models that use either the percolator or drip method. Size is a major consideration—large pots are fine if you want one mostly for entertaining, but the smaller sizes are more efficient for daily use.

Toaster. Look for special features, such as dual controls to make light and dark toast simultaneously; warming cycles or a combination toaster/oven/broiler for making sandwiches. Make sure it is designed for easy cleaning.

Slow cookers. These are ideal for working couples. The electric slow-cooking pot means menus need no longer be limited to dishes that can be prepared quickly after being away all day. Roasts, stews, and sauces can be ready when you come in the door. There are also slow-cooking ovens, so you can prepare a whole meal in eight to ten hours.

Grill (with broil or waffle features). This multipurpose appliance has round-the-clock usefulness in busy households, provides efficient means for quick, hot suppers or late snacks. And little individual hamburger/sandwich-makers fall into this category.

Mixer (standard or portable). Indispensable to anyone who plans to do baking, it beats, whips, and mixes. Now the many attachments on the standard model can include a dough hook. Other featured attachments can include coffee grinders, shredders, grain mills, meat grinders, and blenders. This unit is called a food center. If your kitchen facilities are limited, you may find a small portable mixer adequate.

Frying pan. This is a boon to inexperienced cooks because you can set it to the exact temperature needed for frying, stewing, or braising. There is a setting for keeping foods warm. With a high dome, it can be used for baking.

Deep fryer. Fryer is a misnomer for this appliance, which cooks everything from soup to dessert. Settings are adjustable. Start at simmer—a low heat that's difficult to achieve on a range without good cookware—and go up to the high heat needed for deep-fat frying. Two-cup deep fryers are available.

Food processors. These chop, slice, shred, puree, grate, and are easy to operate and keep clean. They are expensive, but a real friend in the kitchen.

Electric grinding mill. Comes in a variety of sizes; good for coffee, spices, and grains.

Rotisserie. Broils perfect meat and poultry; bastes itself.

Warming tray. This is the answer to the problem of keeping foods hot during serving and eating. Some models have a drawer for warming plates or keeping rolls, pies, and hot hors d'oeuvres.

Blender. This handy appliance takes up little space and performs a variety of services. It chops, blends, purees fruits and vegetables, makes milk shakes and other drinks. For entertaining, you will also want the ice crusher attachment.

Juice extractor. Perfect for a delicious combination of fruit and vegetable juices without waste.

Knife sharpener. If you are getting an expensive carving set for a wedding gift, this is a wise investment. With an automatic device, you can't ruin a knife by oversharpening or uneven sharpening. If you sew, choose one that sharpens scissors, too.

Electric carving knife. For a perfect carving job, an electric knife does the trick. The blades are detachable for easy cleaning. Really outstanding for hard jobs like pineapples.

Electric can opener. Make sure the one you select opens all types of cans you are likely to use frequently—round, oval, square, and extra large. Some have knife sharpeners.

Nonelectric Cookware

Saucepans. These come in various sizes and provide controlled cooking for vegetables, soups, and stews. Most useful are 1-, 2-, 2½-quart sizes.

Omelet pans. For the perfect egg.

Double boiler. When a hot water bath is necessary.

Steamer. For vegetables the perfect health way.

Spaghetti pot. Doubles for stews, stocks, and soups.

Additional Equipment

The housewares department of your favorite store is burgeoning with gadgets that can contribute much toward making your life in the kitchen easier and more pleasant.

At first you'll need only a few of the most important. You can add others as your interest in cooking increases. Most gadgets are relatively inexpensive and you can collect them at a rate equal to your enthusiasm.

To start off, protect the pots and pans you have chosen by purchasing several wooden spoons with which to stir without scratching. A peeler is one of those little musts for fruits and vegetables. A pastry brush is useful for spreading melted butter or beaten egg on pastries, and you should have a pair of tongs for turning chops, chickens, and other foods. Forks should not be used, for they puncture the meat and allow valuable juices to escape. A wire whisk for sauces or dressings can turn an amateur into a professional overnight.

Several rubber spatulas are handy for folding in egg whites and scraping mixing bowls clean. And no cook should lack a pepper mill. Freshly ground pepper is much more pungent than the ground varieties. For other freshly ground seeds and spices you'll need a small mortar and pestle or an electric mill—a functional addition to your kitchen. Some are beautifully designed. A sturdy metal corkscrew is a "can't live without."

Nice equipment to have, but not vital, are: a wire salad basket for shaking excess moisture out of salad greens; an egg slicer to slice eggs uniformly; a cheese grater, such as the Mouli cheese mill, imported from France; cheesecloth for straining aspics; and a melon ball cutter to add festive touches to fresh fruit mixtures. Finally, a pastry bag with several sizes and shapes of tubes belongs in the kitchen of any bride who likes to add decorative touches to salads and cakes or for making fluted borders and rosettes from mashed potato.

OTHER EQUIPMENT

Strainers, large and small tea size; timer; long-handled fork; pierced spoon; serving spoon; potato masher; ladle; spatula; pancake turner; thermometers for refrigerator, freezer, oven, meat, candy; grater; baster; measuring cups and spoons; flour sifter; rolling pin; mixing bowls; colander.

BAKEWARE

Two 8″-square pans; two 9″-round pans; two baking sheets for cookies; Bundt pan for fancy cakes or packaged varieties; muffin tins; six to eight custard cups; two cake racks; loaf pans for cakes or meat; one-quart ovenproof baking dish; three-quart oven-proof baking dish.

The Cookbook Shelf

No kitchen is complete without at least one good cookbook. In addition to any favorites you may have yourself, perhaps based on the cuisine of a particular country, these are highly recommended: *Joy of Cooking* by Irma Rombauer and Marion Rombauer Becker; *Classic Italian Cookbook* by Marcella Hazan; *New York Times Cookbook* by Craig Claiborne; *Making of a Cook* by Madeleine Kamman; *Cooking with Helen McCully Beside You* by Helen McCully; *Book of Great Desserts* by Maida Heater; *Kitchen Tricks* by Ben Charles Harris (tuck this away on your shelf—it has those handy tips for annoying or perplexing situations in the kitchen).

Other marvelous additions to your kitchen library are the inexpensive paperback editions now available. Even if you find only a few great recipes in each, they are worth the price. Another good investment is a metal file box for index cards—your own personal cookbook where you can keep recipes clipped from newspapers and magazines or shared with you by relatives and friends.

Stocking the Shelves

Part of the first day in your new home will be devoted to a trip to your local supermarket. You may have to make more than one trip, or enlist the cooperation of your husband, if you are going to have to carry home enough supplies to begin housekeeping. Many markets have a delivery service that you may wish to take advantage of during the first few days of stocking your kitchen. Plan to spend some time in the market to familiarize yourself with how the products are grouped and where each category is located. You will also want to inspect the meat, vegetable, and dairy counters to be sure that produce is fresh and stored under ideal conditions. You will only want to buy the bare essentials on your first day's shopping. You have many other things to attend to and, besides, it is going to take more than the average amount of your food budget to get started. Additional ingredients can be accumulated over a period of weeks or even months.

A WELL-STOCKED PANTRY
General

*Butter or margarine	Oil
*Milk	Corn syrup
*Cream	Chocolate: cocoa and bitters

*Eggs
Cereal
Sugar: granulated, brown,
    confectioners'
Baking soda
Cream of Tartar
Shortening
Bread
Jelly, jam
Canned foods
Evaporated milk
Soups: especially Cream of
    Chicken, Mushroom,
    Tomato, Potato, Asparagus,
    and Split Pea—any one of
    these, teamed with cooked
    meat, fish or poultry,
    vegetables, and a starch
    base such as rice or
    pasta, can make an
    exciting casserole. They're
    also handy for sauces.
Broths: chicken and beef
Gravies: beef and chicken
Seasonings, condiments, beverages, bottled foods
Prepared mustard
Ketchup
Mayonnaise
Chili sauce
Club soda or carbonated water
Assorted soft drinks

Salt and pepper: seasoned
    and plain
Coffee and tea: instant and
    regular
Hot chocolate mix
*Lemons
Potatoes
Onions: fresh and dried
*Salad greens

Fruits: assorted
Assorted vegetables,
    including these
    basics:
    tomatoes
    tomato paste
    tomato sauce.
Beans: chic peas, red
    and white kidney
    beans—for hot and
    cold salads.
Mushrooms
Boiled onions
Canned fish and shellfish
Worcestershire sauce
Liquid pepper sauce
Garlic: fresh and powdered
Assorted herbs and spices
Dried green pepper, onion
    flakes

Vinegar: wine and cider
Bottled salad dressings
Parmesan cheese
Freeze-dried shallots,
chives

White and red wines, for
cooking
Cooking sherry
Lemon juice

Dry and dried foods
Pasta: noodles, macaroni,
spaghetti
Rice
Cornmeal
Beans
Gelatin: flavored and plain
Crackers
Crumbs
Raisins, prunes, apricots

Puddings
Cake and pie crust mixes
Dehydrated soups
Packaged salad-dressing
mixes
Instant nonfat dry milk
Sauces and gravy mixes
Bread and pastry mixes

Nibblers
Chips and crunchies, assorted
Toast rounds or squares
Crackers, assorted
Olives and pickles, assorted
Pickled vegetables

Nuts, assorted
*Cheeses
*Carrots and celery (always
ready for fresh, crisp,
low-calorie snacks)

Sweets
Cookies, assorted
Jams, jellies, preserves
Mints

*Indicates refrigerator or freezer storage.

THE HERB AND SPICE SHELF

Oregano, rosemary, basil, tarragon, and bay leaf were well known to our forefathers, yet by the twenties these herbs were scarcely used by any but professional chefs. Fortunately, for all of us, the public appetite has once more been sharpened for herbs, and today an impressive list of herbs, spices, and seeds are available at local grocery stores and supermarkets, and a well-stocked herb and spice shelf is taking its place in thousands of American kitchens beside the salt shaker and pepper mill.

Successful seasoning is an art, and herbs and spices must be added with a knowing hand to enhance a dish and not overpower it. Certain seasonings have an affinity to certain foods, yet fail to improve others. Basil, for example, is particularly well suited to almost any cooked tomato dish, salad, aspic, or soup. An herb bouquet, that tiny bundle consisting of a spray of parsley, a pinch of thyme, and a piece of bay leaf, known in early Roman times as a faggot, improves almost any stew. Rosemary is a perfect complement to lamb or poultry. Both tarragon and dill are exquisite with eggs, fish, and poultry and make delicious additions to soups and sauces. Nutmeg is particularly good with creamed chicken or spinach, while ginger complements beef and duck, and mace is perfect with fish.

Fresh dill is often available in the fall months, during the pickling season. If not, the dried dill, known as dill weed, makes an admirable substitute, providing it is bright green in the jar when you buy it, otherwise its strength and flavor are gone. Dill is one of the most popular herbs in Scandinavian countries where it is used to flavor and decorate poached fish and is added to meat balls and loaves. Try adding chopped fresh dill (use sprays, not stems) to a green salad or to sour cream as a dip for vegetables.

Season to taste makes a lot of sense when it comes to using herbs, for some are fresh and some are dried, some are old and some are new, and some, both fresh and dried, have more strength than others. The flavor of herbs and spices diminishes with age, so buy them in small quantities and store them in tightly closed containers and be sure to keep them far away from the heat.

A list of a few herbs, spices, and seeds. Some you will need for basic cooking and baking; others can be added gradually. A fun idea is to buy and try a new herb or spice each month.

Allspice	Mint
Basil	Mustard
Bay leaves	Nutmeg
Caraway seeds	Oregano
Cardamom, ground	Paprika
Cardamom seeds	Parsley
Cayenne pepper	Peppercorns
Celery salt	Poppy seeds
Celery seeds	Poultry seasoning
Chili powder	Red pepper flakes
Cinnamon, powdered and stick	Rosemary
Cloves, powdered and whole	Saffron
Coriander, powdered and whole	Sage
Curry powder	Sesame seeds
Dill weed	Tarragon
Garlic powder	Turmeric
Ginger	Thyme
Marjoram	Vanilla beans

In addition, if possible, it is nice to have a bottle of brandy handy and one or two liqueurs to add their fragrance to cooking. Dark rum is also delightful to flavor desserts.

TERMS USED IN COOKERY

A la king. Food, usually chicken or sweetbreads, served in a rich cream sauce, often flavored with sherry.

A la mode. The addition of ice cream as a garnish for pies and cakes. Also applied to some braised foods.

Almondine. Foods, chicken or fish usually sautéed, garnished with shredded blanched almonds toasted in butter.

Aspic. A well-seasoned clear jelly made from stock, broth, or tomato juice.

Au gratin. Food creamed and baked or broiled until top is brown. Surface frequently sprinkled with buttered bread crumbs or cheese.

Au jus. Meat served in its natural juice, thickened with butter.

Bake. To cook in the dry heat of an oven. Applies to all oven-cooked foods except meats, which are oven-roasted.

Barbecue. To roast meat over coals or on a spit. Also applies to broiled meats served with a barbecue sauce.

Baste. To pour liquids over food while it is cooking or roasting. Such as syrup over baking apple, or pan juices over roasting meat.

Bavarian. A rich pudding containing cream and gelatin.

Beat. To blend by lifting mixture rapidly up and over with fork, spoon, wire whisk, rotary or electric beater.

Bisque. A rich cream soup usually of fish or seafood.

Blanch. To parboil or dip in boiling water, generally to loosen skin from almonds, tomatoes, peaches.

Blanquette. A savory stew with a white sauce.

Blend. To combine two or more ingredients thoroughly.

Boil. To cook in a liquid, usually water, which bubbles actively during the cooking period.

Bombe. A rich frozen cream or custard.

Bouillon. Clarified soup stock.

Bouquet garni. Contains thyme, parsley, and bay leaf; tied together for easy removal.

Braise. To brown food in shortening and then cook, tightly covered, with a small amount of liquid.

Bread. To dip food into egg/milk mixture, then into crumbs.

Broil. To cook under or over direct heat.

Broth. Liquid in which food has been simmered.

Brown. To cook a food by frying, toasting, broiling, or baking, until brown.

Brush. To spread thinly with a pastry brush, usually melted butter or beaten egg.

Candy. To cook in sugar or syrup until transparent and glazed.

Canapé. An appetizing mixture spread on a small base of bread, toast, or cracker.

Carmelize. To heat sugar until light brown in color and caramel in flavor.

Charlotte. A creamy gelatin dessert that is molded with cake or ladyfingers.

Chop. To cut in small pieces with a sharp knife.

Clarified butter. Melt butter over low heat. Remove foamy top (casein) and spoon off deep yellow liquid butter; can be stored.

Combine. To mix ingredients together thoroughly.

Compote. Fruit stewed in sugar syrup.

Condiment. Any food seasoning such as spice, vinegar, relish, or spicy sauce.

Confectioners' sugar. Sugar ground to consistency of flour.

Court bouillon. A highly seasoned broth for poaching fish.

Cream. To mix soft shortening and sugar with a spoon or with an electric beater.

Creole. A highly seasoned tomato sauce containing green pepper, garlic, and chopped onion.

Croquettes. A mixture of chopped or ground cooked food bound with thick cream sauce, dipped into egg and crumbs and fried.

Crouton. Cubes of bread toasted or fried crisp, used to garnish soups and other dishes.

Crumb. To cover with fine crumbs.

Cut. To divide with knife or scissors.

Cut in shortening. To work cold shortening into flour with pastry blender or two knives.

Demitasse. A small cup of strong, rich after-dinner coffee. Literally, "half-a-cup"—usually indicates espresso.

Deviled. Highly seasoned food.

Dice. To cut into square pieces.

Dissolve. To mix a dry substance with liquid until it becomes a solution.

Dot. To scatter bits of butter or shortening over surface of dish to be cooked.

Drawn butter. Melted butter used as a sauce.

Dredge. To coat with flour or sugar.

Drip. Procedure of making coffee with filter method top.

Drippings. Residue left in pan in which food has been cooked and fat removed.

Dust. To sprinkle lightly with flour or sugar.

Egg and crumbs. To roll food in crumbs or flour, then into beaten egg and finally in crumbs; used to prevent fat soaking into foods, or to form a crisp surface.

Eggs, to separate. Break egg shell carefully in half, let white run into a separate container.

En brochette. Food cooked or served on a skewer.

Entrée. The main dish of an informal meal or a dish served between main courses of a formal dinner.

Espagnole. A basic brown sauce.

Fillet. A boneless piece of fish or lean meat.

Fines herbs. A combination of finely chopped herbs such as parsley, tarragon, chives, and chervil in equal parts.

Flambé. To pour warm brandy or liquor over food, ignite, and let flame burn out so alcohol taste is removed.

Flake. Separate into small pieces.

Flour: Use unbleached all-purpose flour in recipes unless otherwise specified.

Fold. To combine ingredients carefully with an up and over folding motion.

Fondue. Melted to sauce consistency, such as cheese.

Frappé. Sweetened fruit juice frozen to a mush.

French. To trim meat away from the end of a bone, such as lamb chop, or to cut into thin slivers, such as green beans.

Fricassee. To stew fowl or meat and serve in thickened broth, often with dumplings.

Fry. To cook in hot fat; when small amount is used, process is known as pan frying; when food is partially covered with fat, process is known as shallow frying; when surrounded with hot fat, process is known as deep frying.

Frizzle. To cook very quickly in a small amount of hot fat.

Garnish. To add a decorative something extra to a dish to make it more attractive.

Glaze. To cover food with a glossy coating such as jelly, mayonnaise, or fruit or meat juices.

Goulash. A thick stew of meat or poultry.

Grate. To rub through a grater.

Grill. To broil.

Grind. To put through food chopper using fine, medium, or coarse blade.

Hollandaise. A sauce of butter, egg yolks, and lemon juice.

Julienne. To cut into narrow lengthwise strips.

Kippered. A method of preserving fish, usually herring.

Knead. To fold and press dough with palms of hands.

Lard. To cover meat with strips of fat, or to thread strips of fat salt pork through lean meat with skewer or larding needle.

Leavening. Ingredients needed to make mixture rise, such as baking powder, soda, yeast.

Macédoine. A mixture of fruits or vegetables.

Marinate. To let stand in a sauce to improve flavor.

Mash. To beat or press to a soft pulp.

Mask. To cover with a mayonnaise or cream sauce containing gelatin or with a clear jelly.

Melt. To heat a solid to liquid form.

Mince. To cut or chop very finely.

Minestrone. A thick vegetable soup.

Mirepoix. Cut in ¼-inch cubes.

Mix. To combine ingredients, usually by stirring.

Mocha. A flavor combination of coffee and chocolate.

Mousse. A mixture containing beaten egg whites, baked, chilled, or frozen.

Nesselrode. A sweet dessert or sauce containing chopped fruit and chestnuts.

Pan broil. To cook in frying pan over high heat.

Pan fry. To fry quickly in small amount of fat.

Parboil. To partially cook in boiling water.

Pare. To remove skin or rind with sharp knife.

Parfait. A dessert of ice cream, fruit, and whipped cream served in a parfait glass.

Peel. To remove skin.

Percolate. Method of making coffee.

Petits fours. Small iced cakes.

Pickled. Foods preserved in brine of salt and vinegar; sugar and spices are often added.

Pilaf. Rice cooked with butter, onion, and spices.

Planked. Food, usually fish or steak, served on a wooden board or plank made especially for the purpose.

Poach. To cook in liquid below boiling point (simmering).

Pot roast. Method of cooking less tender meats in heavy pot with tight fitting cover.

Preheat. To heat oven to desired temperature in advance of baking or roasting food.

Puree. Press food through a sieve to obtain a thick pulp.

Ragout. A savory stew.

Ramekins. Individual baking dishes.

Render. To remove the fat from meats by heating slowly at low temperature.

Reduce. To reduce amount of liquid by boiling off part of the liquid in steam.

Roux. A smooth blend of fat and flour used to thicken a liquid.

Sauté. To cook slowly in small amount of fat.

Scald. To heat liquid to a temperature just below boiling point or pour boiling water over food.

Scallop. To bake food in an oven-proof dish.

Score. To make shallow slits across surface with a sharp knife.

Scramble. A method of cooking eggs, or mixture containing eggs, by stirring over low heat while thickened.

Sear. To brown food quickly on all sides on top of the stove or in the oven.

Shred. To cut or tear in thin pieces, or press through a shredder.

Sherbet. A frozen mixture of fruit juice often containing beaten egg whites.

Shortening. Any kind of cooking fat or oil.

Sift. To put dry ingredients through a sieve.

Simmer. To cook in liquid just at or below the boiling point.

Skewer. To fasten meat with a thin wooden or metal pick.

Sliver. To cut into very fine strips.

Steam. To cook over or surrounded by steam.

Steep. To let stand in hot liquid.

Stew. To cook in liquid below the boiling point.

Stir. To mix with a circular motion.

Stock. Liquid in which meat, fish and/or vegetables have been cooked. Used to make soups, sauces, and gravies.

Stuffing. A mixture of bread or crackers, usually flavored with onion and spices.

Toast. To brown by direct heat or in a hot oven.

Toss. To mix lightly by lifting with fork or fork and spoon.

Whip. To beat rapidly in order to incorporate air.

Table of Measurements

OVEN TEMPERATURES

Slow oven	275°-325°F. or 135°-163°C.
Moderate oven	325°-375°F. or 163°-191°C.
Moderately hot oven	375°-425°F. or 191°-219°C.
Hot oven	425°-475°F. or 219°-247°C.
Very hot oven	475°-500°F. or 247°-261°C.

SIZE OF CANS

No. ½	7¾ to 8½ oz.	Approximately 1 cup
No. 300	13½ fl. oz.	Approximately 1¾ cups
No. 1	1 lb.	Approximately 2 cups
No. 303	1 lb. or 15 fl. oz.	Approximately 2 cups
No. 2	1 lb. 4 oz.	Approximately 2½ cups
No. 2½	1 lb. 13 oz.	Approximately 3½ cups

WEIGHTS AND MEASURES

Pinch or dash	Less than ⅛ teaspoon
1 teaspoon	⅓ tablespoon
3 teaspoons	1 tablespoon
2 tablespoons	⅛ cup
4 tablespoons	¼ cup
5 tablespoons plus 1 teaspoon	⅓ cup
10 tablespoons plus 2 teaspoons	⅔ cup
12 tablespoons	¾ cup
16 tablespoons	1 cup
2 cups	1 pint
2 pints	1 quart
4 quarts	1 gallon
16 ounces	1 pound
1 fluid ounce	2 tablespoons
16 fluid ounces	1 pint (2 cups)

METRIC SYSTEM

Weight

1 ounce=28.4 grams

16 ounces=454 grams or .454 kilograms

2.2 pounds=1 kilogram

Volume

1 tablespoon=1.5 deciliters

1 teaspoon=.5 deciliters

1 fluid ounce=3 deciliters

1 quart=.95 liter

1 gallon=3.8 liters

1.06 quarts=1 liter

1 cup=237 milliliters

EQUIVALENTS

Ingredient	Quantity	Equivalent
Butter	1 pound	2 cups
	1 stick	½ cup
	½ stick	4 tablespoons
Chocolate	1 square	1 ounce
Cheese	1 pound	4 cups, grated
	4 ounces	1 cup, shredded
Cream	1 cup	2 cups, whipped
Dates	1 cup, chopped, pitted	About 6 ounces
Eggs, whole	5	1 cup
	1 large	¼ cup or 2 ounces
Egg yolks	16	Approx. 1 cup
Egg whites	8 to 9	Approx. 1 cup
Flour, bread, sifted	4 cups	1 pound
Flour, cake, sifted	4½ cups	1 pound
Green peas	1 pound	1 cup, hulled
Lemon	1, squeezed	2 to 3 tablespoons
Lemon rind	Rind of 1 medium	2 tablespoons, grated
Macaroni	8 ounces, raw	5 cups, cooked
Meat	1 cup, ground	Approx. 8 ounces
Noodles	8 ounces, raw	5 cups, cooked
Nut meats	1 cup, chopped	4 ounces
Pecans	2½ pounds in shell	3 cups, chopped nut meats
Potatoes	3 medium	1 pound
Rice	2⅓ cups, raw	1 pound

Rice, whole grain	8 ounces (about 1 cup)	4 cups, cooked
Onions	3 medium	1 pound
Shortening	1 pound	2⅓ cups
Sugar, brown	2¼ cups, firmly packed	1 pound
Sugar, granulated	2 cups	1 pound
Sugar, confectioners'	4½ cups, sifted	1 pound
Tomatoes	3 medium	1 pound

SUBSTITUTIONS

Ingredient	Substitute
1 square (ounce) chocolate	3 tablespoons cocoa plus 1 tablespoon shortening.
1 tablespoon cornstarch	2 tablespoons enriched flour.
1 cup fresh milk	½ cup evaporated milk and ½ cup water or 3 tablespoons nonfat dry milk solids and 1 cup water.
1 cup sour milk	1 cup fresh milk and 1 tablespoon lemon juice or vinegar.

ABBREVIATIONS OFTEN FOUND IN COOKBOOKS

Gal.	Gallon	Tsp., t.	Teaspoon
C.	Cup	Tbsp. T.	Tablespoon
Oz.	Ounce	In.	Inches
Pkg.	Package	Min.	Minutes

Pt.	Pint	Sq.	Square
Lb.	Pound	Qt.	Quart

HOW TO MEASURE

Use standard measuring cups and spoons and be accurate.

Measuring liquids. Glass measuring cups with graduated markings and lip for easy pouring should be used for liquids. Hold glass level with eye to make sure liquid comes to desired amount.

Dry measure. Use the nested unit measuring cups and standard measuring spoons. Fill to the top and level off with straight-edged knife or spatula.

Flour. If recipe calls for sifted flour, this means to sift before measuring; presifted flours have eliminated this step in baking.

Brown sugar. Pack firmly into dry measure cup and level off.

Shortening. This can be measured by displacing water. If ½ cup is specified, fill liquid measure ½ full of water, then add shortening until water reaches the 1 cup mark. Pour off water and remove fat, which will not stick to sides of cup.

HOW TO BE A GOOD COOK

1. Read recipes carefully. Assemble ingredients and utensils.

2. Make necessary advance preparations before beginning to cook, such as mincing an onion, dicing celery. In France this is called *mis en place*—everything in its place—and many chefs have assistants who do nothing but prepare the mis en place for the master chef, who then takes over. If the two of you plan to take turns cooking, you might also take turns at being the assistant.

3. Be accurate.

4. Preheat oven to degree specified.

Chapter 11
Your Own
Audiovisual
Center

There's no place like home for enjoying some of the best entertainment the world has to offer. Films, sports events, theater, and live up-to-the-minute news right at home on T.V. — in color if you wish. And on the music scene there is high fidelity to set the mood.

Yes, in the fast-paced world of electronics, there is always something new on the market to increase your enjoyment of sight and sound. For most newlyweds, consider starting off with the basics, but keep your eye open to the future when you may wish to add on or trade up to something more sophisticated as taste and circumstances change.

Before you shop or request electronics equipment as gifts it helps to familiarize yourself with what is available and to understand the terminology used by sales personnel or seen in advertisements and manufacturers' brochures.

Two Types of Systems

There are two main types of high fidelity systems. One is the *compact* system, the other the *component* system. With a *compact* system you get all of the parts — radio receiver, player, and pair of speakers — all wired, assembled, and ready for you to operate. All you need do is insert the plug. You need do no wiring of your own.

In this setup, one speaker is placed to your left and supplies sound normally played on the left side to center stage. The other speaker, on your right, covers the remaining half of the stage. The sound section of an orchestra is regarded as consisting of two channels of sound — left and right. A stereo receiver is often called a two-channel receiver, but you will also be listening to monophonic sound, or mono. A solo speaker or solo singer without accompaniment is mono. But whether mono or stereo, all sound will come out of both speakers. The simplest compact unit will have just a receiver and two speakers, while a more elaborate unit will also have either a record player or record changer. More expensive compact high fidelity units will also play tape.

The term "compact" may be misleading. Some are small and others as large as a television console. If your compact has external speakers, place them eight feet apart for best stereo sound.

A *component* high fidelity system is much more sophisticated than the compact type, for you must select not only individual units — receiver, speakers, record player, and tape recorder player — but you must be sure they will all work together. Since these are frequently made by different manufacturers, be certain all can be successfully combined. You will also need to connect the components by wires, which is not as difficult as it seems at first glance. Finally, a component system is almost always more expensive than a compact — and unlike compacts, which may be housed in attractive furniture units, individual components look highly functional.

However, the component system is usually preferred by real high fidelity enthusiasts. With such a system you can add more components as your budget permits. There is no question, either, that a component system does supply superior sound because the speakers are not housed together with all the other parts, allowing you to position them for best stereo sound.

When buying separate components, shop for each individual unit, making sure it is the best available within your budget. You're safest if you rely on brand names. Get as much literature as possible on the components you are interested in buying. Find out from your dealer if components can be traded in when you are ready for something more advanced in equipment.

The Sound of Music

If you were born with a good ear for music or are gradually developing an appreciation for the finest in stereophonic sound, you will want to investigate some of the latest advances in equipment and think about acquiring them.

Sound engineers who design equipment for the home are striving to reproduce what you hear in the acoustically perfect halls of the most famous concert and opera halls—and they are getting closer all the time.

When you attend a concert, the sound not only reaches you from musicians on the stage, but also travels, bouncing off walls, ceilings, people, and seats. Not all the sound reaches you at the same time and, for some reason, this adds to its beauty, giving it depth. In an auditorium, you are literally bathed in sound, enjoying the combination of sound that comes to you directly and sound that is reverberated or bounced off the walls and other surfaces. Stereo or two-channel sound is only direct, and so isn't a true representation of what you hear at a concert. Quadraphonic or four-channel sound is an attempt to add reverberated sound to direct sound. A quadraphonic component system contains parts that do just that.

If you have an existing component stereo system, you can change it to four channels by adding one more component called a decoder, another pair of speakers, and one more stereo amplifier. An easier approach is to buy a four-channel receiver. This will contain a four-channel decoder and four amplifiers, so you need only supply four speakers. It's more expensive than stereo, but much more satisfying.

The Advantage of Tape

A great addition to your high fidelity system, and one that can pay for itself in the long run, is a tape recorder. Tape is an electronic blackboard. You can wipe out all or any part of it, then record once again on the same tape.

Use tape to record your favorite discs. You will be able to listen to these selections over and over again without record wear. Borrow records from a library or friends, tape them, and this music is yours for only the cost of the tape.

Tape playing ranges from a convenient thirty minutes to as much as several hours. You can even record a complete opera. Tape is available in three forms—cassette, cartridge, or open-reel. Cassette and cartridge come in small plastic packages, so all you do is plug right into a cassette recorder/player with cassette tape or into a cartridge player for cartridges. The two are not interchangeable.

With cassette and cartridge you never touch the tape. Open-reel is wound on exposed reels. To use cassette tape you will need a cassette tape deck. You can connect this directly to your component high fidelity system, but not to a compact type. A cartridge player may have its own amplifier and speakers. Open-reel tapes are used on open-reel decks wired to your high fidelity component system. Open-reel offers the best high fidelity sound reproduction using tape.

Guidelines for Shopping

These shopping tips will enable you to select a high fidelity system that will give you years of listening pleasure.

1. Components made by different manufacturers often look alike, but aren't. An inexpensive receiver may seem identical to one costing twice as much. To assure quality, buy brand names only, preferably with an Institute of High Fidelity label.

2. When purchasing a high fidelity system you'll often find many options offered. These "extras" can double the cost. It's like buying an automobile. The low end model will perform as well as the loaded-with-extras model, but without as much flexibility. If you may never use the optional equipment, don't buy it.

3. Try to get literature abut the components you hope to buy and read it carefully before making a decision. If you don't fully understand, speak to a friend who is already into hi-fi and have him explain it.

4. Along with price, consider the kind of warranty and the time limit on it. You may pay more to buy from a manufacturer who has

an excellent reputation for quality control plus making good on guarantees, but in the long run it's usually worth it.

5. A "live" demonstration in a showroom usually means little. The record may be worn and the shopping center is probably in a high noise level area. It helps to bring along your own record, one you are thoroughly familiar with and know to be free of scratches and worn grooves.

Housing Your Equipment

The most efficient way to arrange your electronic equipment, and portable television set if you have one and want it in the same place, is in a wall storage system. Be sure this system is wide enough so that you can place speakers the required eight feet apart and that the shelves are deep enough to accommodate the width of parts. If there is no outlet nearby, arrange to have one put in before installing the system. Since high fidelity components are often more functional than beautiful, plan to surround them with enough plants, books, and other accessories to make this wall a decorative addition to your room.

Where to put hi-fi is a matter of how you enjoy listening to it as well as where you have sufficient space. The bedroom may be the place if you've arranged it as a kind of bedroom/den or second living room, and you like to enjoy serious music without conversation or other interruptions. If music is a more social pastime, the best place is the living room where you'll be able to enjoy it with visitors. In either case, study the floor plans you've made. If yours is a complex type of component system, bring your floor plan to the store. The salesman may give some tips on best placement for top sound reproduction.

Glossary of Terms

High fidelity salespeople speak a language all their own and will be throwing these terms at you.

STULUS: this was formerly known as a phonograph needle. *CARTRIDGE:* it holds the stylus in position and converts the movement of the stylus into tiny electrical currents. *TONEARM:* holds and supports the cartridge. Inside the tonearm are wires that carry the electrical signal from the cartridge to an amplifier. *PRE-AMP:* abbreviation for preamplifier. It strengthens the electrical signals from the cartridge. *POWER AMP:* abbreviation for power amplifier. After being treated by the pre-amp, the signals are led into a power amp where they receive a great boost in electrical energy. *SPKRS:* abbreviation for speakers. *WOOFER:* a speaker designed to reproduce bass tones. *TWEETER:* a speaker designed to reproduce treble tones. *SQUAWKER:* a speaker designed to reproduce midrange tones. *S/N:* abbreviation for signal-to-noise ratio. A comparison between signal (which we want) and electrical noise (which we don't want). Tuners and receivers are plagued by electrical noise from fluorescent lights, motors in home appliances, etc. These noises can ruin your listening pleasure. The higher the s/n, that is, the greater the amount of signal compared to the amount of noise, the more you will like what you hear. *BASS:* low frequency tones. *MIDRANGE:* tones that occupy the region between the bass and treble. *TONE CONTROL:* a control on a tuner, receiver, speakers, and amplifiers that lets you adjust the sound of your high fidelity system to your own personal taste. *TUNING METER:* an illuminated meter on the front of a receiver or tuner. It helps you tune in a broadcast signal for maximum signal strength. Proper tuning improves the signal-to-noise ratio. *MODE:* a switch on the front panel of a tuner or receiver that lets you select the kind of musical enjoyment you want. It has a phono position so you can listen to records, an auto stereo position so your receiver will play in stereo, an aux position to let you listen to auxiliary sound sources such as a cassette or cartridge.

Chapter 12
Moving In and Getting Settled

I t might be hectic, but it's also fun to move into your new home and anticipate the way it will look when you are really settled, with everything just the way you have always imagined it would be.

To bring the dream a lot closer to reality, get yourself organized now. In addition to planning the actual moving day and being ready for it, be prepared for all the little tasks associated with making a house a home, then keeping it in good order.

First Home Moving Hints

FUNDAMENTALS

There are certain matters to deal with well in advance. Make sure that all utilities will be turned on in your new home—gas, electricity, and water. Arrange for telephone installation. Choose your locations and the type of instruments you would like. Insurance against fire and theft should become operative the minute your belongings are moved in. Engage a mover and get his advice on any special problems. Plan for the furnishings you have bought to be delivered on fixed days when you or someone can be there to direct where they go. Rugs, obviously, should be delivered and laid before the furniture arrives. If you and your husband subscribe to magazines, notify them of your change of address. Also notify your post office. Change addresses on owners' and drivers' licenses. If you are planning to pack certain things yourself—books, records, linen, clothing, and so on—start saving cartons—the ones groceries come in.

THE ACTUAL MOVE

There are three ways to move, two of which involve employing a good, reliable, and experienced moving firm. In the first way, the movers practically do it all. They pack everything from a grand piano to an ash tray (including clothing) and install all of them in your new home so that all you have to do is walk in and start enjoying it. This is, obviously, the easiest and also the most costly way to move.

The second differs only in that you deal with packing such things as linen, clothing, books, records, pots and pans, appliances, and so forth. Fragile items—lamps, ornaments, mirrors, pictures, china, glass—and all furniture, bedding, and rugs are left to the moving men. Of course, if you are good packers, you can handle fragile things yourselves and, thus, economize by being set to go when the men arrive. Number cartons and identify the contents therein. Then you can instruct the movers to place certain numbers in various rooms. They charge by the hour for each man, so it's to your advantage to be really ready for them. In any event, be sure the moving company arranges for an insurance policy to cover your valuables in transit.

As an alternative, you can hire a trailer or moving van from a rental agency and do it all yourself. This seems economical, but may cost more in the long run if you break or damage anything and are not insured. Unless most of your furnishings are newly purchased and are being delivered directly to the new address, think twice before you take on this big job yourselves.

China and glass. In packing these and other fragile objects, you will need barrels (often available from your moving company), cartons of various sizes, and unlimited old newspapers and excelsior or shredded newspaper. To pack china and glass, first put a thick layer of excelsior (or shredded newspaper) in the bottom of a barrel; then wrap heavy objects such as bowls or platters individually in layers of newspaper and fit them in snugly. Remember, the heavy objects always go at the bottom; and the more delicate the object, the more padding and layers of newspaper it requires. Pack in a second layer of excelsior and then a circle of plates, each separately wrapped and each standing on edge. Be sure there is plenty of excelsior between any object and the inner side of the barrel. Cups, each one wrapped by itself, can fill in the center as can small glasses. Then add another layer of excelsior pushed in all around and among, then a layer of smaller objects and so on until the barrel is filled. Top it off with more excelsior. Remember, the aim is to protect each object from its neighbors.

Lamps and ornaments. These should be wrapped in newspaper, too, and bedded in excelsior in strong cartons or barrels. Lamp shades should be wrapped in tissue paper and packed in large cartons so they cannot shift.

Silver. Your silver is probably almost all new and still in its protective flannel. That's the way to pack it, but, since it isn't breakable, you will not need so much excelsior. The exception is hollow pieces, which must be protected against dents.

Books and records. These should be packed in *small* strong cartons so that the weight of each will not be excessive. Place books with bindings back to back. Records should be packed upright and exactly fit their containers.

Soft objects. Towels, blankets, and certain clothing—sweaters, lingerie, and so on—may be packed in furniture drawers, but table and bed linens are too heavy for this. They should go in cartons that allow them to lie flat but that are not too large, because of the weight factor.

Toilet articles. Pack these among the soft things, but beware of spillable cosmetics that might cause damage. Wrap them in tissue and pack them upright in a small carton.

Pots and pans. These and other kitchen equipment should be wrapped and packed like the other objects above with the heaviest things at the bottom. Mops and brooms may be tied together and moved separately.

As you pack, mark. Use either a grease pencil or gummed labels and mark on the outside of absolutely every box exactly what it contains. This may seem time-consuming, but just wait until you want to get breakfast for the first time in your new home and where, oh, where is the percolator! Of course, if the moving man or your mother has unpacked and put everything away, this problem won't arise, but think of the trouble you'll be saving them if everything is identified.

Your special needs. You may find that some of the information above does not apply to exactly what you need to have done. But, if you will pick out the basic things that concern your own problem, we're sure you'll move easily and without tears.

Arranging Everything in Place

Once the moving men have left and most of the cartons have been unpacked, your home should be fairly livable, but as yet lacking the personal touches and little grace notes that add up to a lived-in look. Here's where both of you step in—with a big assist from a set of hand tools that neither home owner nor apartment dweller should be without.

In the weeks that follow moving day, much of your spare time will be taken up with hanging pictures and mirrors, installing towel bars and drapery rods, perhaps adding another clothes pole to the closet, and assembling and installing the wall unit you purchased for the living room. Minor incidents may also occur, from stopped-up drains to leaky faucets, that you may find are less frustrating when you have the tools to fix them at once yourselves rather than tracking down a landlord or building employee.

Hand and power tools proliferate in hardware stores to the point where it is difficult to narrow down one's needs. But unless you own your own home or rent a house with garage, basement, or tool shed, these are good for starters.

FIRST HOME TOOL KIT

Sixteen-ounce claw hammer, one end for driving nails, the other for pulling them.

Two screwdrivers, for Phillips and flat-head screws.

Pliers, for grasping nuts or cutting wire.

Crescent wrench, for loosening nuts and bolts, changing sink washers, etc.

Hand saw, for cutting lumber.

Square, for measuring when cutting with a saw.

Level, to assure straight surfaces.

Six-inch ruler or metal tape for measuring.

Awl, to get holes started for screws in plaster or Sheetrock.

Hand or power drill, with set of assorted bits, for drilling holes in metal or hardwood.

Stud-finder, for locating studs behind walls.

Flashlight and candles, for power failures.

Plunger, also called plumber's helper, for suctioning out matter clogged in sinks and bowls.

Boxes of assorted size nails, screws (Phillips and regular), nuts and bolts, toggle bolts, and washers for sinks.

Electrical tape.

Picture wire and hooks.

Guidebook for home repairs. There are many excellent books, many in paperback editions, that give instructions on minor repairs you can do with the above tools. They also tell what to do until the plumber, electrician, appliance or heating repairman arrives. Look for one with a very complete index and keep it handy, as you would a first aid book to go with the supplies in your medicine cabinet.

Having these basics on hand before you move in is a good idea because you are going to need many of them right away. Gradually, you can acquire additional tools necessary for more complex carpentry. Meanwhile, when expensive tools that will be used only occasionally are needed, it's better to rent than buy.

KNOW WHERE EVERYTHING IS

As soon as you move in, or beforehand, if you have the chance, have the owner or an employee take you through the apartment and acquaint you with the operation of fuse boxes, heating and air conditioning systems, and so on. Find out if there are separate shut-off valves for water entering each sink, toilet bowl, and tub. If so, you are in luck—you can shut off any one of these in case of an overflow or if repairs are necessary. If you rent an apartment in a private dwelling rather than an apartment house, ask the owner to show you where main shut-off valves and electrical systems are located and also to give you access to the basement in case of emergencies that occur in his absence.

Much of what you will be doing in the beginning, of course, involves attaching things, both decorative and useful, to walls and windows. The chart on pages 184 and 185 indicates what kind of hardware and tools are required for items of various weights attached to plaster, Sheetrock, wood, brick, or tile.

Keeping Your House in Order

After you are settled in your new home, you'll want to work out a routine for keeping everything in good order, yet without becoming a slave to your possessions. With so many other demands on your time, housekeeping is something that can and should be dispensed with as quickly as possible.

Just as cooking is a lot easier than it used to be, cleaning is much simpler, too. Furniture and floors with no-wax finishes, self-cleaning ovens, frost-free refrigerators, wash-and-hang curtains, wash-and-wear clothes, and a long list of other improvements have made it possible to be away from home all day and still get the necessary work done. But when you are trying to make every minute count, having some kind of routine, however flexible, is a help.

SETTING UP A SCHEDULE

In modern marriage, the tendency is to share cooking, cleaning, laundry, and shopping chores as equitably as possible so that both

ITEM	PLASTER
Pictures, mirrors, clocks, and other wall accessories up to 100 pounds.	Use conventional picture hooks in correct size for weight you are hanging. To avoid chipping plaster, put a piece of masking or cellophane tape over area where nail will be inserted and hammer gently. For heavy mirrors and other items 50 pounds or more, locate the studs* and nail to them a piece of plywood ($\frac{1}{4}''$ by $3''$ by width of item). Then nail picture hooks to plywood.
Book shelves supported by bracket arms.	Best procedure: locate studs,* then secure the metal strips to the studs with wood screws. If studs cannot be located, substitute toggle bolts for wood screws.
Towel bars, tie racks, knickknack shelves and other items supporting light weights.	Use long self-threading screws (at least $1\frac{1}{2}''$).
Wall-hung furniture.	Locate the studs.* Affix cabinet to studs with lag screws ($2''$ to $3''$ long). If studs cannot be located, use toggle bolts.
Curtain and drapery rods hung from wall or ceiling.	Use self-threading screws.
Curtain and drapery rods hung from window jambs.	For wood jambs, use wood screws. For steel jambs, affix rods to surrounding plaster or Sheetrock whenever possible. If not possible, drill into jamb with electric drill and use sheet metal screws.

SHEETROCK	WOOD PANELING	BRICK OR TILE
Same as plaster, but protective tape not necessary.	Use conventional picture hooks or wood screws.	For brick, obtain steel-cut nails and nail them into the mortar. For tile, or brick that has been plastered over, use a masonry or star drill to make openings for lead expansions shields.
Same as plaster. If studs cannot be located, substitute Molly bolts for wood screws.	Use self-threading screws (¾″ to 1″ long).	Same as above.
Same as plaster.	Same as plaster.	Same as above.
Same as plaster. If studs cannot be located, use Molly bolts.	Locate studs.* Affix cabinet with wood screws (1½″ to 2″ long). If studs cannot be located, use self-threading screws at least 1½″ long.	Same as above.
Use Molly bolts.	Use self-threading screws.	Same as above.

*To find studs, rap on wall, moving along until you detect a change in sound from hollow to solid. The stud is behind the solid area and others are usually spaced 16″ apart. Or, buy a stud-finder at the hardware counter—a magnetic device that points out studs by attracting nails.

husband and wife are free to grow as individuals. There are two ways of doing this: either tasks are divided and permanently designated, or they alternate from week to week—this week is yours for laundry and next week you take over dishwashing in its place. In either case, have some kind of routine and a written reminder so each of you knows what has to be done each day. Keeping up with daily tasks makes cleaning easier. Most things require only a once-over-lightly, if done often enough, and your weekends will not be spent digging yourselves out of a mess rather than enjoying the things both of you look forward to all week.

To make up a simple work chart, analyze your housework patterns over a period of a week or two. Then make three lists—for jobs that should be done daily, weekly to monthly, and occasionally. Study the lists and see how you can rearrange jobs to save steps. Try grouping together those that require the same equipment or are located in the same area. Schedule weekly cleaning tasks on logical days for each operation, like defrosting the refrigerator the day before doing the weekly marketing.

The following suggestions on daily, frequent, and occasional cleaning tasks provide a basis for making up your own schedule. These suggestions are intended as guidelines only. How much cooking you do, how much time you spend out of the house, and even the amount of air pollution in your neighborhood are all factors that determine how often various tasks need to be done.

Daily or two or three times a week. Swab the kitchen floor with a mop wrung out of hot soap or detergent suds. Wipe the range burners and refrigerator with a sudsy sponge. Empty trash baskets and replace paper liners.

Dust and tidy rooms if needed. Vacuum or carpet sweep and use a dry mop on uncovered floors.

Wash the bathtub, basin, and toilet with ammoniated cleaner.

Wipe the bathroom floor with a mop wrung out of suds.

These tasks, of course, are in addition to the essentials—dishwashing, bedmaking, marketing, and cooking.

Once a week. Clean the kitchen floor with warm suds, rinse and mop up excess moisture, wax if necessary. Clean the range thoroughly, inside and out. When needed, defrost the refrigerator, remove contents and wash with baking soda inside and out. Wash trash and garbage containers with hot suds and scalding rinses.

Vacuum upholstery, draperies, blinds, window and door frames, rugs, floors, and baseboards. Vacuum or brush fabric lamp shades. Swab plastic shades with a sudsy sponge.

Clean the bathroom, scrubbing or mopping the floor thoroughly and scrubbing down tile walls to remove soap and mildew.

Polish some silver and other decorative metals so that all of it won't have to be done at once. Swab railings and doorknobs with a sponge. Wash mirrors and glass tabletops. Polish wood furniture.

Occasional chores. Remove contents of closets. Wash floor, walls, and fittings with a sudsy sponge. Empty drawers, wipe clean, and reorganize contents.

Shampoo upholstery and rugs. Launder washable curtains, draperies, and slipcovers.

Vacuum the walls. Wash the kitchen walls with soap or detergent suds.

Wash wood floors, woodwork, blinds, and furniture. Wax or polish those surfaces that require it.

Empty, wash, and rearrange cabinets, medicine chests, cupboards, and shelves.

Wash light bulbs, window shades, and fabric lamp shades with warm suds.

Suds-sponge flower pots and the leaves of houseplants. Wash the windows.

Housecleaning Equipment

The right equipment will greatly facilitate housework. The items listed on the following pages are necessary in every home.

FLOOR CARE

Although you can get by with one vacuum cleaner for now, it's nice to have two—a lightweight for quick pick ups and a heavy-duty cleaner. Which vacuum cleaner you should buy depends on three considerations: how large your home is; what type of coverings you have or want—thick shag, wall-to-wall, area rugs, low-pile carpeting, or a lot of exposed hard floors; and what you expect your cleaner to do for you.

Upright vacuum cleaner. This is generally the heavy-duty cleaner. The principle of cleaning is beating the dirt out of the rug with the vibration of the beater bar and sucking it up into the bag with air. If you are selecting an upright, look for carpet, flooring height adjustment. It's a good thing to have optional attachments to clean above the floor.

Canister vacuum cleaner. This is definitely the most versatile cleaner for bare floors and carpeting. There are many models with attachments and speeds for above the floor cleaning. When looking for a good canister, try it in the store. Check horsepower rating. The canister works by air suction. Today there are many combination canister cleaners with two motors—one at the end of the wand to give upright cleaning power in addition to one in the canister itself. Check for additional features—cord rewind, amount of accessory items, and push buttons for suction control.

Handy attachments. A dusting brush is perfect for woodwork, window sills, books, blinds, bric-a-brac. The crevice tool is for hard-to-reach places—under and in between; furniture brush is for mattresses, upholstery fabrics, and draperies; floor brush vacuums floor without scratching.

Lightweight vacs. Designed for quick, efficient pick ups, this is a perfect supplementary cleaner for daily use and decidedly more efficient than a broom.

Rug shampooers and floor polishers. Some of these come as one unit capable of shampooing carpets as well as waying and polishing floors. This taskmaster is ideal for the twice-a-year carpet shampoo, once-a-month waxing, and weekly buffing for a shiny, perfectly polished floor.

Washing and waxing floors. A good general rule is to wash the floor with a brush or mop wrung out of soap or detergent suds to avoid excess moisture, then wipe speedily with an almost-dry cloth or mop. Never apply wax until floor is completely dry. Note the following tips for specific kinds of floors.

Asphalt tile: mop with warm suds and rinse.

Concrete: scour with a stiff brush and hot suds. Flush-rinse with hose if the floor has a drain.

Cork tile: wash with warm or cool suds and rinse. Wax as desired.

Hardwood (shellacked or varnished): wash at intervals with warm suds. Rinse and mop dry quickly, never letting water stand.

Linoleum: wash at least once a week with warm suds and rinse. Wax if desired.

Painted: wash with warm suds, rinse, and dry quickly.

Vinyl tile: wash with cool-to-warm suds, rinse, and dry promptly. Some plastic tiles are best left unwaxed, so follow manufacturer's instructions for daily and occasional care.

Spot cleaning rugs. For best results wipe up spills immediately. Be sure to pretest all solvents recommended. The following methods will help you remove specific stains:

Food, starches, sugars: remove excess by blotting up with clean absorbent towel or scraping. Sponge lightly with cool water and blot. Apply diluted detergent or wool wash. Rub gently, rinse with sponge, blot, and let dry.

Oily materials and grease: blot up excess. Apply a spot cleaner. Know your fibers first. Wash with diluted rug shampoo. Let dry and vacuum.

Alcohol-base antiseptics and perfumes: remove excess. Sponge with alcohol and water. Keep repeating until stain color is absorbed. Use clean white cloth or towel. Then apply carpet shampoo. Let dry and vacuum.

Cigarette burns: for light burns, brush area lightly then carefully clip away charred tufts. Shampoo. Severe burns will need repair or replacement.

Glue, model: after removing excess, carefully apply nail-polish remover by drops to soften glue. Scrape or blot away. Then shampoo, let dry, and vacuum. Remember to pretest nail-polish remover as it may affect some synthetic fibers.

Gum: after removing as much as possible by scraping, "freeze" the residue with ice cubes in a plastic bag. Break or scrape off brittle gum. Shampoo, let dry, then vacuum.

Mud: scrape up as much wet mud as possible and allow residue to dry completely. Vacuum well, then shampoo. Let area dry and vacuum again.

Nail polish: after removing excess, apply nail-polish remover by drops to soften, then blot or scrape away. Shampoo, let dry, then vacuum. Remember to pretest polish remover as it may affect some synthetic carpet fibers.

Paint, oil base, wet: after removing excess paint, carefully apply turpentine or paint thinner and blot repeatedly. Shampoo, let dry, then vacuum.

Urine: blot up excess with clean towel. Sponge with cool water and blot. Then sponge with white vinegar and blot well. Shampoo, let dry, then vacuum.

Water: for severe wetting, mop or blot as much as possible. Dry carpet quickly to prevent rot or mildew. Once dry, shampoo lightly, let dry, then vacuum.

Wax, candle: remove excess by scraping. Cover with several layers of paper toweling and press lightly with a warm iron until all wax is removed. Be careful not to melt fibers with iron. Shampoo, let dry, then vacuum.

Doing the Laundry

BASIC STEPS

1. Sort carefully by color. Always wash permanent press and synthetic fibers as separate load. They easily transfer color. Sort linty fabrics and wash away from dark fabrics if linty fabrics are dark or vice versa. Towels are lint givers.

2. Pretreat stains and heavily soiled areas.

3. Select correct washing temperature.

4. Use right type and amount of laundry detergent or soap.

5. If washer has cycles, follow instructions.

6. Don't overload. Clothes won't be as clean.

7. When using dryer don't use a too hot temperature. Remove permanent press immediately.

WATER CONDITIONERS

If a scum forms, then water may be hard. This scum causes dulling and laundry takes on a grey cast. A water softener in wash or final rinse is recommended.

BLEACH

This should always be added to the washing machine along with the detergent in the wash cycle.

Chlorine bleach should not be used on wool, silk, acetates, and spandex. Read label to see if bleach contains chlorine. Measure bleach with accuracy. Don't pour bleach on clothes. This can cause damage. To add bleach to washer, dilute first with at least one quart of water. Some machines have an automatic liquid bleach dispenser. Follow manufacturer's instructions for its use.

Oxygen bleaches are safe for most washable fabrics and can be added directly to wash water.

FABRIC SOFTENERS

There are a variety of fabric softeners on the market. Their purpose is to reduce static electricity. Add to the final rinse. To prevent staining clothes, dilute with water.

FABRIC CARE

To insure laundering success, buy washables. Save and refer to manufacturer's instructions on hangtags or labels that come with purchases. Here are general rules to guide you in deciding what and how to launder.

Blends of fibers should be washed by the method prescribed for the dominant fiber.

Cottons, linens, and rayons are machine-washable in hot suds and rinses if white or colorfast; warm suds if colors are doubtful. All but the most delicate cottons can be machine washed, but consult labels as some need special care, such as cottons treated with resin finishes for soil- and crease-resistance.

Silks may be washed by hand or machine in warm suds and rinses. Press with a warm iron while still damp. Avoid sprinkling, which can cause water spots. If fabric becomes dry, wrap in damp towel to distribute moisture evenly before pressing.

Stretch fabrics may be hand or machine washed in warm suds and rinses. Drip or dry automatically at low heat. Replace stretch covers on furniture while they are still damp.

Synthetic fiber fabrics, such as Dacron, Dynel, nylon, and polyester are machine-washable. Check labels to determine proper time settings for sturdy or delicate materials. Cool-to-warm water helps prevent creases, but does not remove deep-set soil or wrinkles ingrained by wear. Therefore, it is advisable to use hotter water for every fifth or sixth washing, followed by a cool rinse before the first spin to minimize wrinkling.

Water-repellent finishes are machine-washable unless otherwise stated on hangtags or labels. Use warm suds and extrathorough rinsing. Pressing with a cool iron tends to renew the effectiveness of the finish.

Wools are best washed by hand unless pretreated for shrink-resistance. Use lukewarm suds and rinses, keeping in mind that this fiber is very absorbent and requires more suds than other materials. Lay flat to dry, or place in automatic dryer at AIR.

Dishwashing Tips

As we all know in this machine age, dishwashers are considered wife savers. Washing stacks of dishes is definitely boring, time-consuming work. Dishwashers are producing hygienically clean results. Less handling results in less breakage. They also use less water when washing capacity loads once a day. To save electricity, look for dishwashers with an energy saving button to avoid the heat on the dry cycle. Some dishwashers have rinse and hold cycles for small loads. Some have pot scrubbing and soak cycles.

There are some items that should not be washed in a dishwasher. Plastics should definitely be marked dishwasher safe or the heat will ruin them. Other plastics can stain from chlorine bleach in dishwashers.

Cookware is generally safe, but, if there are wooden handles, the dishwasher is not the place for them. Copper and brass would be better off washed by hand. Iron skillets are best wiped off with a soapy damp sponge. They are most effective when oil seasoned (usually described by manufacturer). So avoid dishwashers here. Some aluminum may spot or darken from the hot water.

Most stainless steel flatware and sterling can be washed safely in a dishwasher.

If glassware has a cloudy appearance after dishwashing, this may be caused by either a soil or a mineral hardness. This can be treated by using a water softener such as Calgon or Calgonite for dishwashers. Read the packages of detergents carefully for built-in softeners. There are also rinse aids for dishwashers.

The proper order is crystal and glassware first. Rinse and place on drainer rack. Next, the flatware—place in drainer cup. Let everything drain well. Never use terry towels on glassware. They are too linty and glassware is best when dried with linen. The dinnerware follows; pots, pans, and cooking utensils are last. Always stack carefully in drainer rack to avoid chipping.

Tip: tea and coffee stains can be removed with baking soda.

General Housecleaning Hints

Today's bride sets up housekeeping in a washable world. A home and its contents, with few exceptions, can be kept clean with water and soap or detergent suds, plus some of the cleansers for specific tasks. Time-tested cleanliness methods are listed alphabetically.

BATHROOM

Wash tile or painted walls, or plastic-coated wallcovering with cloth or mop wrung out of hot suds; rinse with damp cloth. Mop or scrub floor, cleaning between tiles by dispensing a solution of suds and bleach from a squeeze bottle along the grout. Go over fixtures with sudsy sponge, removing stains with scouring powder. Pour hot suds and bleach in toilet bowl before scrubbing with long-handled brush. Bathtub rings can be prevented by adding a spoonful of detergent to the daily bathwater.

CURTAINS

To test for soil, hold several folds of the fabric together. If this reveals dinginess not visible on a single layer, the curtains need washing. A second clean sudsing is advisable, since curtains literally "sieve" soil out of the air. Most fabrics used for window dressing today are no-iron as well as washable and can be hung back up while still damp.

Dacron, nylon, and Orlon may be washed by hand or by machine after putting them into a mesh laundry bag to prevent snags and "roping." Use warm suds and rinses, and hang without wringing to drip dry, or use a dryer. To wash these synthetics by hand, use warm suds in bathtub or deep sink. Lightly fold the curtains into quarters, immerse, press suds through with palms of the hands, then rinse the same way. This avoids rubbing or wringing that could cause deep creases.

Fiberglass may be machine washed only if so stated on the manufacturer's directions. After washing and rinsing, blot in a towel, then rehang, smoothing hems with fingertips. *Rayon* may be handled like nylon, using a cool iron and pressing lengthwise when fabric is nearly dry. *Cottons* are machine-washable in warm suds (for colors) or hot suds (for whites) and may need no ironing if dried in a dryer. Four to six average-size pairs make a load.

FURNITURE

Wood, use "dry" suds (made by beating a handful of soap or detergent with a little water until the mixture peaks like meringue), applied with a soft cloth, to remove soil and old wax or polish from wood surfaces. This thorough cleaning is needed occasionally even by the finest antiques. Wash with the grain of the wood—haphazard motions leave streaks. Rinse with an almost-dry cloth, then rub with completely dry cloth, always using the same methodical strokes to enhance the pattern. If possible, use a wood block, of pine or other soft wood, to stroke wood surfaces after rinsing. This smooths down any fine "hairs" that have been raised by moisture. A piece of an old orange crate will serve as a block. Only when furniture is thoroughly dry should the appropriate oil or wax finish be applied.

LAMPS AND SHADES

Bases of ceramic, glass, glazed pottery, plastic, metal, and wood can be wiped clean with a sudsy cloth, rinsed with a damp cloth, then wiped dry.

Bulbs should be removed from sockets to wash the glass with a sudsy cloth, but never wet the metal neck. Dry before replacing.

Cords should be disconnected and drawn taut through a sudsy cloth or sponge, then wiped and allowed to dry completely before being connected.

Shades may be sponged clean with "dry" suds or immersed in sudsy water, depending on material and construction. Coated fabric, plastic, paper parchment, or parchment shades should be given the "dry" suds treatment, rinsed with damp sponge or cloth, and wiped dry. This method is also recommended for fabric shades that are glued. Stitched fabric shades may be plunged into deep warm suds, using sponge or soft brush on stubborn spots. Rinse in clear water, or use a spray. Shake off excess water and dry in a current of air or near an electric fan.

Reflectors may be put into hot suds, rinsed, and wiped dry.

Indirect lighting fixtures may include luminous ceilings, wall brackets, cornices, and valances—with plastic panels, corrugated sheeting, frosted glass, louvers, or other translucent shielding. All need regular washing in warm suds. Plastic panels are lightweight and easy to remove from suspension bars. Corrugated plastic in sheets may be unfastened, rolled, and carried to a large washtub or bathtub. Do not use abrasives on plastic—a soft cloth or sponge wrung out of suds is safest. Let plastic "air dry" before replacing, because rubbing creates static electricity that acts as a magnet for dust. Wearing soft white gloves while handling plastic panels will prevent leaving fingerprints.

METALS, DECORATIVE

Aluminum may be washed with warm-to-hot suds, scoured with fine steel wool if needed. Rinse with hot water, dry, and polish with a soft cloth.

Brass, if lacquered, should be washed in lukewarm suds, rinsed, and rubbed dry. Badly tarnished unlacquered brass needs hot suds followed by polish when dry. A piece of lemon dipped in salt, or hot vinegar and salt, will remove corrosion. After polishing, wash again thoroughly.

Chromium, needs only warm suds and rinses, followed by polishing with a soft cloth.

Copper should be washed in warm suds. Add a little ammonia to remove spots caused by corrosion. Rinse, dry, and apply polish.

Pewter normally comes clean with warm suds. If heavily tarnished, cover with silver polish; then, while still wet, apply suds, generously. Rinse in hot water and dry thoroughly.

Silver, when used regularly, stays bright simply through hot sudsing and rinsing. Polish is needed only occasionally. If ornamental, polish at regular intervals after washing. Use clean soft cloth to buff.

Stainless steel responds promptly to washing in hot suds, as deposits of all kinds come off easily. Use a well-lathered sponge, fiber brush, or cloth; then rinse and wipe dry.

When metal objects are being stored for any length of time, wrapping them securely in plastic wrap will retard tarnishing by keeping them fairly airtight. Oxidation is what causes tarnish to form. Any metal object benefits from regular polishing. If neglected too long, pit marks will form that are difficult, if not impossible, to remove.

OVEN CLEANING

If you have a standard oven, there's only one way to clean it. And you're it. There are a variety of commercial cleaners on the market in aerosol cans. When spraying, never do so near an open flame. The cleaner can be highly corrosive when used in presence of high heat or open flame. Great damage can be done to the porcelain enamel finish, painted finish, or bare metal. The temperature for the product to work at best is 200°F.

The simplest way to keep your oven clean is to:

1. Keep up with soil after each use. Always wash broiler after each use. This eliminates that dreadful, strenuous job everyone loathes.

2. If there are one or two drip spots after food is removed from oven, and it cools down a bit (200°F.), place a cloth soaked in ammonia on spot for about thirty minutes. Soap and water should remove soil.

3. For easy care, heat oven to 200°F. and place a pan of ammonia in oven overnight. Wipe up soil next morning.

4. For heavy soil, a little steel wool and soap is all right.

If you keep up with oven grease, the torturous task will definitely be removed.

FOR A CONTINUOUS-CLEANING OVEN

A continuous-cleaning oven has oxidizing agents applied to the liner. The surface coating feels like little peaks and valleys to the touch. Oxidizing agents and expanded surface help dissipate grease and soil while oven is in use. The effectiveness of this oven is determined by higher temperatures and length of time in use.

GENERAL RULES FOR CLEANING THIS TYPE OVEN

1. Wipe with nylon pad or sponge, plain water. Blot dry and run oven for two hours at 475°F.

2. Never use commercial cleaners. They can ruin the finish.

3. Never use metallic soap pads, steel wool, scouring powder, or an abrasive cleaning agent. Residue left behind can interfere with cleaning mechanism.

4. Avoid heavy spillover by using a cookie sheet or aluminum foil on bottom surface. If using a gas range, be sure not to cover vent holes. If a heavy spillover occurs, first blot up excess, and wash off with water while still warm. When oven has cooled down, use an all-purpose/wipe-off cleaner. Use a plastic net pad to rub in cleaner. Leave on about fifteen minutes. Rinse with cool water until clean. Run oven at 475°F. for two hours.

SELF-CLEANING OVEN

The self-cleaning oven works by literally burning off food spills. It leaves nothing behind but white ash.

Here are some general guidelines for using this method:

1. Before using self-clean cycle, wipe interior with damp cloth. This wipe up will help avoid smoke from incinerating process.

2. Remove racks after cleaning process and wash in sink to remove a bluish color taken on by cleaning.

3. The oven frame and door liner must be wiped before cleaning cycle. These areas are not reached in automatic cleaning.

4. If oven is not completely clean, the cycle may have been too short. Next time lengthen cleaning time.

5. Never use a corrosive cleaner in this type of oven.

PLANTS

Swab dust and soot from foliage with sponge or cloth wrung out of cool soapsuds. Rinse in same manner, protecting earth in pot with a sheet of plastic or waxed paper slit at one side and fitted around plant stem. Or turn the pot upside down and dip foliage into suds, then into rinse water, holding plant firmly in place. An atomizer may be used to apply sudsy solution and rinse water to very delicate foliage. Swab plant containers with sudsy sponge, rinse, and wipe off excess moisture. Allow plants to dry away from sunshine. Apply mineral oil to make leaves shiny.

PLASTICS

Many plastic items, such as tablecloths, shower curtains, and raincoats, can be washed by machine with towels added to the load as buffers. Use warm suds and rinses, short cycles, and remove as soon as the washer shuts off. Hang to drip, wipe dry, or use a dryer at OFF or lowest heat setting. Plastic draperies, slipcovers, and bedspreads can be washed "on location"—sponge the surface with suds, rinse with a clean damp cloth, and wipe dry. Because plastics are nonporous and nonabsorbent, soil is easily removed. So, between machine washings, a quick going over with suds is effective, using a brush to clean soil from textured surfaces.

POTS AND PANS

When presoaking, use cold water for utensils containing residues of milk, eggs, starchy foods; hot water for sugary or greasy residues. Washing directions are as follows:

Agate and enamel. Handle gently, treating as glass. Wash only with hot suds as abrasives encourage chipping. If food is burned on, soak in suds until crust can be scraped off with a rubber or wooden spatula.

Aluminum. Wash in hot suds, using steel wool if necessary to remove discolored spots. Scald and wipe dry.

Chrome. Wash with hot suds, rinse and wipe dry, polishing with soft cloth.

Copper. Wash in hot suds, rinse, dry carefully with soft cloth. If badly soiled, apply a paste of hot vinegar, salt, and flour in equal parts, allow to dry, then wipe off. Follow by sudsing, rinsing, and drying thoroughly to restore the original luster.

Glass. Wash with hot suds and rinses. Never use coarse abrasives. Air dry or wipe with soft cloth.

Iron. Use hot suds, and a stiff brush or steel wool if necessary. After rinsing, wipe completely dry.

Nickel. Wash in hot suds, rinse, and rub dry with soft cloth. Prompt and thorough drying will prevent water spots.

Electric cookware. Many newer items may be submerged in hot suds for thorough washing. Follow manufacturer's directions carefully, however. If the electrical unit is not detachable, the appliance should not be completely immersed in water.

RANGES

Wipe up spills as they occur. Use a sudsy sponge or cloth to wash enamel surfaces daily, when cool; rinse and wipe dry. Wash removable parts—drip pans, broiler racks, oven shelves, burner grates or reflectors—in deep hot suds at the sink. Rinse and dry thoroughly before replacing. Electric units will burn themselves clean; gas burners should be removed for sudsing with a stiff brush. Wash deep-well cooker with hot suds after each use. Swab inside of oven with sudsy sponge; if grease has collected, leave a bowl of suds and ammonia in the cooled oven overnight to loosen the deposit. After this is wiped away, wash again. Or, use one of the many chemical products, some of which are left overnight.

REFRIGERATORS

When needed, defrost, remove food and shelves, and swab the interior with a sudsy sponge or cloth. Wipe with damp rinse cloth. Put removable parts such as shelves and containers in deep hot suds and wash ice trays in warm suds. Rinse thoroughly and dry all parts before replacing. Wash the rubber door seal and go over inside surfaces with a sudsy sponge. Even if your refrigerator defrosts automatically, it still needs this weekly cleaning to get rid of stale food odors.

SALAD BOWLS

Contrary to some theories, wooden salad bowls can be washed, but should not be soaked. Use warm suds and rinses, then wipe dry. When bowl is thoroughly dry, rub in coating of oil and let it remain overnight. Then wipe with paper toweling until all oily residue is completely removed.

SHOWER CURTAINS

Launder often, by hand or machine. An easy way is to swish through warm suds and rinses in the bathtub. If badly soiled around hem and edges, use a soft laundry brush. Rehang on shower rod to dry, weighting hem with skirt hangers.

SLIPCOVERS AND DRAPERIES

In general, cottons and linens, and white and pastel colors can take hotter water than synthetic fabrics, deep tones, and prints. Synthetics, and natural fibers treated with stain-resistant and wrinkle-resistant finishes, require warm suds.

Slipcovers. Shake, brush or vacuum to remove dust and lint. Close zippers or grippers. Rub thick suds into soiled spots and let set for ten minutes. Wash one large or two small pieces per machine load. Or, soak briefly in a tub, then use a plunger for sudsing and rinsing. Dry by machine or hang over parallel lines. In either case, remove covers while still slightly damp and replace on furniture. Stretch seams and welts, pull pleats into place, and smooth flat areas. Set an electric fan nearby to complete drying.

Draperies. Follow manufacturer's instructions on whether to wash by hand or machine. When hand washing, do one panel or one pair at a time, in deep laundry tub or bathtub with plenty of room to swish them through suds and rinses. After drip drying over parallel lines, or machine drying, remove slightly damp and press at once. If pressing is optional, rehang at windows and stretch edges and seams. In machine washing synthetic fiber fabrics, keep both wash and spin cycles short.

TABLE LINENS

It is wise to launder new table linens before using to remove the factory finish, soil, and finger marks due to handling, pasted labels, machine oil, or embroidery stamping ink. Don't try to use them just once more before laundering. Any food or beverage stains should be pretreated at once. Then cloth and napkins can be laundered later when convenient.

Many plastic and plastic-coated cloths can be machine washed, so follow manufacturer's directions. Always press "real" linen quite damp with a hot iron—first on the wrong side, then on the right for luster. To reduce wear, change the fold lines from time to time when storing linens. Or roll them on cardboard cylinders to eliminate creases.

UPHOLSTERY

If the fabric can safely take water, it can be shampooed with "dry" suds applied to upholstery with rotary motions. Wash small sections at a time, overlapping strokes and scraping off soiled suds with dull edge of a knife as you work. Then rinse with clean cloth wrung out of clear water. Wrap cloth around a ruler to work suds into crevices between seat and back and along arms. Rinse with same method.

VENETIAN BLINDS

Dust or vacuum, then tilt slats down and wipe with cloth or sponge wrung out in warm suds. Rinse with clean damp cloth and repeat with slats turned up. Occasionally, remove blinds and immerse in deep warm suds. Scrub tapes on both sides with a well-lathered brush. Rinse, wipe, and let blinds hang full length while tapes are drying, to prevent shrinkage.

WALLS AND WOODWORK

Most wall finishes can be safely washed with soap or detergent suds. If in doubt, test with sudsy sponge on hidden area.

Painted walls. After dusting with wall mop, apply thick suds with sponge or cloth—one section at a time, with overlapping strokes. Rinse with sponge wrung out of clear water, and wipe dry. Change to clean suds and rinse water as needed. Always work from the baseboard up to prevent water from dribbling down over soiled walls, leaving hard-to-remove streaks.

Wall coverings. For asphalt, cork, vinyl, and other wall tiles, use same sudsing method as for painted walls. Use also for coated or plasticized fabric and linoleum.

Woodwork. Go over moldings, door and window frames, sills, and cupboards with sponge or cloth wrung out of warm suds. Wash thoroughly to remove gummy old wax, then rinse and allow to dry before applying fresh wax.

WINDOWS

Wash with warm soap or detergent suds, adding a few drops of vinegar or kerosene and a little bluing for extra sparkle. A bottle brush dipped in suds will pick up dust from corners of windowpane molding. Rinse with warm water and polish dry with lintless cloth.

WINDOW SHADES

Spread washable shade flat. Scrub with stiff suds and sponge or brush, using overlapping strokes on one section at a time. Rinse-wipe with clean damp cloth, avoiding excess moisture. After completing one side, turn shade and wash reverse side. Rehang at window, leaving unrolled to dry thoroughly.

Chapter 13
Buying Guide for
Very Important Purchases

lanning a first home is a headlong plunge into the buying spree of a lifetime. Never before have there been so many important purchases to make in a short time.

Since many of the major items you are about to select will be in daily use for many years to come, a little knowledge about each of them is well worth having. You can't become an expert on everything overnight, but you can learn to seek out quality and use common sense to make sure you are getting the most for your money.

Fortunately, "Let the buyer beware" is an old axiom that need not apply to anyone who shops in stores of good reputation and looks for labels of well-known manufacturers. In the long run, the seller who deals in shoddy merchandise or misrepresents his products has more to lose than the buyer, but to avoid frustrating, time-consuming hassles, steer clear of all but quality merchants who are anxious to win you over as lifelong customers.

Shopping expeditions run a lot more smoothly when you've done some homework first. Telling a sales clerk you want to buy a mattress, for example, doesn't give him much to go on. Be prepared with specifics—a king-size, extralength, innerspring mattress, for example. In the furniture department, it helps to know popular styles by name—and, of course, to have your floor plans with you.

As your purchases are made and delivered, remove care and cleaning hangtags, guarantees, sales receipts, and other information. File these away together in a special place so you can refer to them as needed.

How to Buy Furniture

Even if you've never shopped for furniture, you can invest your money wisely just by using good judgment and looking for the telltale clues that indicate quality. To help decide on the type of furnishings you want, look at the styles on display in the furniture department. It isn't necessary to be an expert on names, dates, and places of origin associated with Early American or French Provincial in order to know whether or not you like it, but it is helpful to have a general idea of what is available.

THE FURNITURE STYLES

Early in this book you learned about the general four-way classification of furniture styles used in the home furnishings industry —traditional, provincial, Early American, and contemporary. Briefly summarizing these: Traditional has a regal air, since it embraces reproductions of actual court furniture. Occasionally named for the original designer, such as Sheraton, it is more often identified by the reigning monarch of periods when these designs were created, literally, to the king's or queen's taste. Decoration is generous in traditional pieces, and ornate signatures include gilt, paint, carvings, fretwork, claw-and-ball feet, and extravagant fabrics. Curved or straight-backed chairs, tables, lowboys, desks, and other pieces often feature the cabriole leg—a gracefully curved knee that is one of the most familiar trademarks associated with traditional furniture.

Provincial furniture—French, Italian, and the others—is the result of the frank envy of the outlying provinces where craftsmen tried to duplicate the designs of the court in local and less expensive woods. Provincial inherits the grace, charm, and form of court pieces, but eliminates the lavish decoration, thereby achieving a timelessness of design that makes it ideal for today's homes.

Early American traces its origin and practicality to our colonial artisans who shrugged off the idea of decoration and built furniture for practical use by hardy pioneers. This once rugged, now refined, style is currently being translated into casual furniture at home in any room in the house and is very popular among newlyweds and young families.

Contemporary furniture is current design and is a classification that refers to the simplicity of line and modern functional qualities found in today's furniture. These designs offer a charm dependent upon grace of line, and decoration is usually inherent in the piece—a beautiful wood grain or inlay, perhaps, rather than something added on for purely decorative value. Actually, modern furniture dates back to the designs of 1925—a period of experimentation from which evolved a whole new school of thought. You may buy a beautiful piece advertised as "Danish modern," but do drop the modern and call it contemporary instead.

After style, the next most important factor is the type of wood your furniture is made from.

CHOOSING FURNITURE WOODS

Hardwoods, which come from leaf-bearing trees, are best for furniture construction. You will find six fine hardwoods prominent in the styles popular today. Although many woods may be stained or bleached to any color tone, the natural blonds are fine-grained birch and maple. Birch—strong, sleek, and generally blond, but sometimes finished in soft brown for contemporary pieces—is moderately priced and a favorite with young couples. Maple is white to pinkish brown naturally, but best known for the reddish finish created for Early American furniture. In the browner tones, too, maple is beginning to develop as a popular contemporary design wood.

Mahogany and walnut are the aristocrats of woods and, hence, the most widely imitated. True mahogany, a rich brown wood imported from Africa, Central America, and the West Indies, offers the very finest wood figures. So-called "Philippine mahogany," on the other hand, is not mahogany at all, but a term applied to a whole group of woods that is imported from the Philippine islands.

Walnut, the cabinetmaker's ideal, is used for every type of furniture except Early American. It is not heavy, but extremely strong, and its natural brown color may be bleached or finished to any tone desired.

Cherry is popular for both provincial and traditional furniture. Characterized by a rich and vibrant reddish brown color and an interesting soft grain pattern, this hardwood is the only true fruitwood now in general production, although you may see an occasional piece with pearwood accents.

Making a comeback in the fashion world of woods is oak—coarsely grained in appearance and sturdy in performance. Practically indestructible, oak is excellent for ranch-style furniture.

While these are the woods you will see most often when shopping for furniture, there are, of course, many other varieties, such as rich and exotic teak that is popular in Scandinavian furniture and favored by so many contemporary designers.

FURNITURE FINISHES

In finishing, the natural wood tone is either carefully maintained, deepened to a darker hue, or lightened to achieve a new effect. This treatment enhances the natural grain and gives more lasting beauty to hardwoods. A final coat of lacquer, rubbed again and again, covers the surface to bond in the color and protect the wood. Lacquered furniture needs only a semiannual paste waxing to keep it lovely. Some pieces are finished with pure linseed oil, and an occasional oiling will enrich the wood's appearance.

THE SHOPPING TRIP

Armed with basic information on furniture styles and woods, you should also know the terminology of the trade before you shop.

You will find furniture woods referred to as solid, veneer, and genuine. Most hardwood furniture you see will be veneered, simply because the lavish grains and figures of these woods are prohibitively expensive in solid form. Veneers make woods even stronger than they are naturally and permit the use of costly woods for general manufacture—a surface layer of a rare hardwood may be attached to a less expensive base wood.

Solid pieces are often made of maple and less frequently of other woods, since a solid piece might be extraordinarily heavy as well as costly. The label genuine indicates the use of the hardwood, such as "genuine mahogany," for veneers on surfaces and in solid form for structural parts—legs and stretchers, primarily. Be sure to look for tags indentifying woods and know what you are buying.

Don't confuse "wood" with "finish." When a piece of furniture is identified as "walnut finish," this usually means a less expensive wood has been colored to resemble walnut, just as the costume jewelry you buy in "silver" or "gold" is merely another metal finished to resemble silver or gold.

Just as important as good materials is good workmanship. When buying a chair, table, chest, or similar piece, rock it to test its steadiness. Inferior furniture may be made of unseasoned wood and loaded with glue in the joints, and you can detect this by its wobbly action. Check drawers for free and easy motion, and look for dovetail joints at front and sides. Ask to be shown the guides and corner glue blocks at the bottom corners of each drawer. Turn a chest or dresser around to check the back. The back panel should be recessed into grooves in the upright posts, not simply nailed flush to the back. Good construction is absolutely essential to assure the longevity of the pieces you buy.

Well-made furniture has proper reinforcement at places of strain, so have the salesman turn over the table or chair you are considering to assure yourself of this safeguard, and query him if you are uncertain about anything. Blocks will be screwed and glued into corners if the furniture is sturdily constructed.

If you are splurging on one or two fine pieces, look for indications of superior workmanship. Drawer tops and insides of drawers should be hand-finished and show the same veneers as exposed areas. Backs should be finished the same as sides and fronts, and back legs of chairs should be as carefully made as front legs. Finishes should be creamy smooth to the touch, and in these expensive pieces you will see the most impressive examples of veneer magic—luxurious figures and skillfully matched wood grains. Do not settle for anything less than exactly what you want in terms of quality of craftsmanship.

All About Upholstery

There's a lot more to an upholstered chair or sofa than meets the eye. The most important features of construction—the frame, webbing, springs, and filling material—are carefully hidden behind a fabric cover.

When buying any item with hidden quality features, it's important that you shop in a reliable store. Few people are gullible enough to buy a television set in a store that may be a fly-by-night operation, yet many will take their chances with furniture merchants whose sensational "bargains" are of mysterious or unknown origin. Before you grasp the alluring price tag that reads "far below original wholesale," let your common sense assert itself.

YOU GET WHAT YOU PAY FOR

First of all, the making of upholstered furniture represents an amazing paradox in this age of mechanization. Although new filling materials, springing techniques, and other advancements have brought about revolutionary changes in style, much of the work is still being done by hand. Today, skilled workmanship is one commodity that is never sold at cut-rate prices. A well-made sofa is an object of pride and able to command a fair price in a competitive market. If the workmanship is there, you have to pay for it, and if it isn't there, you shouldn't buy it.

Learning something about the various steps in construction will enable you to detect certain evidences of quality and to ask the salesman intelligent questions about parts you can't see or touch. First, let's deal with these hidden construction features.

The Frame. Upholstered furniture is usually built around a wood frame. To be strong, the wood should be of fairly substantial lumber that has been kiln-dried (seasoned to prevent warping). It should be put together with dowels and reinforced with corner blocks. In assembling the frame, enough glue must be used so it won't come apart.

Webbing. You've seen outdoor chairs made by fastening strips of webbing material to a simple frame. The webbing technique is also used to form the base for upholstered furniture. The strips are made of some strong fiber, like jute, and often they are interlaced for greater strength. The closer the strips, the sturdier the finished product will be.

Springs. Most furniture is constructed with springs and stuffing in the seat, and sometimes there are springs in the back as well. Good springing lends both comfort and wearability. Contrary to what you may have heard, no one spring construction is superior to all others. Most manufacturers, in fact, use several different methods because the same type spring is not suitable for all furniture styles. The same construction used in a well-padded traditional sofa can't be duplicated in a streamlined contemporary model. In general, the closer together and deeper the springs, the better—an inexpensive chair will have four to six rows of springs; a higher priced chair will have more. Springs should be tied to each other so they will not come apart. Sometimes, springs are found in loose cushions as well as the body of the chair, but today, springless cushions are by far the most popular. A layer of burlap is used to cover the springs, and then the filling materials are added. Some manufacturers have perfected techniques for eliminating springs from seats as well, thanks to tough, bouncy modern fillings that have built-in comfort and durability.

Filling materials. Both the quality of the filling and the amount used are important to the comfort and wearability of the furniture. Almost every state has a law requiring that stuffing and cushioning materials be described on a tag attached to upholstered furniture or bedding. Look for this tag and read it carefully. Among the materials you'll see mentioned most often are hair, foam rubber, polyurethane, down, Dacron, Fortrel, and Kodel.

Hair, or combinations of hair with other materials, varies in quality. Curled or rubberized hair from animals is the best kind. Horse and cattle hair are better than hog hair as they are longer and more resilient. Hair is normally used with a top layer of cotton to prevent prickling. Less expensive are moss; cotton, which is not as resilient as hair and should be used in combination with hair; sisal, a tough grass; and excelsior, the cheapest filling. The better the filling, the less tendency it will have to mat down and make the furniture lumpy, uncomfortable, and misshapen.

Foam rubber is one of the most widely used cushioning materials. Although associated with contemporary furniture because it permits slim styling and crisp lines, foam is also extremely prevalent in traditional upholstery. It is long wearing, comfortable, and has excellent resiliency — the seat bounces back after you get up and it's never necessary to plump up the cushions.

A more recent development is polyurethane foam, which in characteristics and appearance is similar to foam rubber. Polyurethane is lighter in weight and somewhat lower in cost.

Down, very definitely in the luxury class, is wonderful to sit upon and gives a soft look to furniture. While some women object to the fact that down cushions become rumpled and have to be fluffed up, this is the basis of their charm to others. Not everyone admires cushions that never look as if anyone sat on them.

Dacron, Fortrel, and Kodel fiberfill are man-made materials that have a soft look and feel somewhat like down, and they spring back without plumping. They are often used in combination with another core material — as a wrapping around foam rubber or polyfoam, usually, to give a softer line.

WHAT YOU CAN SEE FOR YOURSELF

So much for what's underneath. But, except for the filling materials that must be labeled, what's the good of knowing all this if you can't see it anyway?

First of all, some manufacturers voluntarily attach tags to their furniture describing features of the frame, springs, webbing, and other construction details. If there is no tag, ask the salesman to point out these facts to you.

Now for the features you can see, touch, or test for yourself. Women, many salesmen claim, often overlook the most obvious way of judging quality—that is, by sitting on the furniture to see how it feels. Good springs and quality filling materials give a chair comfort. Next, take off the seat cushion and touch the furniture. If a chair is not well padded, you can feel the springs. Then push down the border of the seat and see if it gives—this will tell you if it has spring-edge construction, a comfort and quality feature. Hard-edge construction, which has no give, is a cheaper technique, although perfectly satisfactory. As for springs and webbing, you could ask the salesman to turn a chair over so you can look at the under side, but the chances are the burlap or cambric dust protector tacked to the bottom will be too heavy to see through. You will have to assume that if the sofa meets other tests, the manufacturer has not stinted on quality inside.

Take a good look at tailoring and other details, just as you would when buying a coat or dress. Does the fabric fit neatly, and, if patterned, has it been carefully matched? Do loose seat and back cushions zip off for cleaning? Is the welting trim and even? Ask if the fabrics are cut on the bias, as this is a technique used by manufacturers to keep cushion covers from twisting.

Finally, consider the fabric. Although looks and color are important, you should give some thought to wearability, since recovering furniture is expensive. Usually you are given a choice of several grades of fabric. It's wise to buy the best grade you can afford, but price alone is not a barometer of quality—some of the silks are expensive but not meant for long, hard wear. Some of the synthetics, like nylon, have remarkable durability. Often, upholstery fabrics are blends of two or more fibers. Many fabrics at modest price levels feature a cotton warp, which is very sturdy, and a rayon or nylon filling. Don't use thinness or bulk as a criterion—a thin fabric may be firmer and stronger than a heavier one. Closely woven fabrics wear better than loose weaves. Fabrics that pull if something catches on them are not practical.

Be sure to ask questions about care—your covers will look fresh and new much longer if you remove spots immediately and follow any other recommendations on upkeep.

How to Buy the Best in Bedding

There are hundreds of tips and gimmicks and gadgets that are supposed to induce sleep. But for most of us, nothing succeeds like good bedding. Here are some pointers to insure you the best value for your money.

Buying the bed itself is a matter of choosing the furniture style you like, but do select a bed that is long enough and wide enough. It should be at least 30 inches wide for each adult sleeper, and long enough so your feet don't hang over. This brings up the matter of double beds versus single. If you decide in favor of a double, there is a strong argument for the extrawidth beds (queen- or king-size) ranging from 60 to 78 inches in width. As mentioned earlier, the standard double bed is 54 inches wide, and when you divide this in two each sleeper gets as much room as he or she would have in a baby's crib. For a compromise you can always combine the best of both worlds and choose twin beds attached to a single head-board. Then, either twin-bed or king-size linen can be used.

DON'T HOPE SPRING'S ETERNAL

As a newlywed you'll want to start married life with a brand-new mattress, but be reasonable about how long it will last. Even the best mattresses get worn out and market experts claim many people are still trying to sleep on them. Some people have an almost marital devotion to their old mattresses and stay by them through thick and thin. If you buy a good mattress, it will be guaranteed to last for many years, costing in the long run no more than a couple of cents a night. Is a good night's sleep worth this price to you? To help you understand why mattresses vary so greatly in price, here are some facts about how they are made.

There are three basic types of mattresses—innerspring, foam, and solid upholstered. As to which is best, it's mostly up to you and the one you like. Innerspring and foam, however, are more popular by far than solid upholstered. The latter are stuffed with cotton, horse or cattle hair. These mattresses get their comfort from the resiliency of the stuffing and the foundation under them. Good hair mattresses are exceptionally expensive and not widely available. Foam mattresses are made from the milk of rubber trees, or a synthetic, which has been treated and whipped up into a foam. They are usually about 4½ to 6 inches thick, considerably thinner than an innerspring mattress, and usually sold in combina-tion with a special box spring that gives the bed the correct height. When you make your purchase, be certain it has a one-piece core and not just foam flakes. Generally, good foam mattresses are expensive. Foam mattresses never lump, sag, or lose their shape and they will support any weight evenly and strongly. But no matter what type of foam you buy, insist on a particularly good spring foundation for support.

The innerspring mattress consists of strong coil springs of steel with insulating material and padding on both sides of the coil unit. A cover or tick encloses the entire unit. There are two types of coil-spring construction. The coils may be sewn into separate cloth pockets, which are joined together, or the coils themselves may be linked together with steel spring or wire. Proper design with innersprings gives a mattress just the right amount of resiliency on the surface, plus a firm supporting core.

VALUES ARE HIDDEN

When you shop for a mattress, you'll see covers beautifully quilted or printed with flowers. But, as for the things that really matter, you can't actually see what you are buying. You can't thoroughly test it either, unless they let you spend the night in the store, although it is recommended that you lie down on the mattress to see if the degree of firmness suits you. Primarily, you will have to rely a great deal on the brand name, the bedding label, the type of guarantee, and the salesman's answers to questions.

As important as the mattress itself is the other half of the set— the spring on which the mattress rests. There are three types of spring foundations—flat springs, metal-coil bedsprings, and the more well-known box springs.

Flat bedsprings consist of flat strips or links of steel spring wire that run horizontally and are attached inside a frame at the sides and ends with helical springs. Spring-wire coil bedsprings are similar to box springs but aren't upholstered or covered with ticking. Double-deck coils are extra long and supported through the middle, and are preferable to single-deck coils. Box springs have steel spring-wire coils mounted to a wood frame base, and the outside of the coil unit is padded and covered with ticking to match the mattress. The coils of better box springs are tied to each other and to their base and border with special twine or wire.

Both box springs and open-coil bedsprings provide an excellent foundation for a good mattress. To get the best comfort and service from whatever mattress you buy, you should also buy the bedspring designed especially for it.

BED LINENS

When you go to shop for linens, know the exact measurements of your mattress since linens tend to vary a great deal in size. Be very careful of buying "bargain" bedding since this often means a smaller-cut-size item that might be more appropriate on a smaller bed. The bottom sheet should completely cover the surface of the mattress plus allowing for a 12-inch tuck-in all around. Pillowcases should be 2 or 3 inches longer and wider than the pillow.

There are several combinations of fibers in sheeting:

Polyester cotton blends. These are the most popular by far, since they do not require ironing and always look fresh and smooth on the bed. These sheets are available today in a vast array of styles, all up-to-the-minute in design.

Nylon or polyester blends. These sheets are strong, easy to wash, and dry very quickly but are far less absorbent than cotton blends, so they need to be changed more frequently. Again, these sheets are also available in numerous designer styles.

Cotton percale. The finest percales have a thread count of more than 180. The higher the count, the softer the sheet. All-cotton sheets are now again available having the attributes of being cool, crisp, and comfortable. However, these sheets are by far the most expensive and lack the convenient no-iron qualities of man-made fiber blends.

Muslin. These sheets are very durable and coarse to the touch and have a much looser weave of cotton fibers. Muslin sheets are by far the most economical purchase.

ADDITIONAL BEDDING REQUIREMENTS

Pillows. Remember that the function of a good pillow is to lend support. There are generally two sizes, the standard and the king, and these will come in various degrees of hardness or softness . . . a matter of individual preference. The polyester pillow is the most popular and is also great for allergic people. The latex foam pillow provides good, firm support, and is also nonallergenic and washable. (Protect your foam pillows from the sunlight since the sun tends to damage the structure of the foam.) Pure down pillows are the most luxurious, and also the most expensive, so a good compromise would be a combination of feather and down if this is your preference.

Blankets. Blanket warmth comes from the thickness of the fabric and the height of the nap. The nap is formed by thousands of little curls that make air pockets . . . these are the real secret of keeping warm. Your blanket will keep you warm just as long as the nap remains. Quality is your best protection. Remember it is the air, not the weight, that creates warmth, and two lighter blankets might be better than one heavy one because there will be a layer of air between them.

The best blankets you can buy are wool, synthetics such as Orlon and Acrilan, or a mixture of wool and synthetics. The synthetics launder especially well and are strong and durable requiring a minimum of care.

The electric blanket is great for extra warmth . . . for example, in an unheated bedroom or a damp house. It takes the cold dampness out of the bedding if turned on shortly before you retire. Be sure to select a blanket with a thermostatic control...preferably, dual controls for the double bed. Choose from reputable manufacturers and stores, once again, who will stand behind their products and guard against fire hazards.

Comforters and quilts. A lot of people today are choosing the beautiful new comforters or quilts instead of, or along with, the blanket, for warmth. The new comforters and quilts are manufactured by the sheeting companies to coordinate with their current sheeting designs...so this can be a wonderful way to coordinate your bedroom simply. They are especially pretty if you have skirted your bed with a matching bed ruffle.

Continental quilts. The new continental quilts are versions of the old-fashioned feather bed of yesteryear. They come in mixtures of polyester, or down and feather combinations—the polyester one being washable and nonallergenic. The continental quilt saves on bedmaking since it eliminates a need for tons of other blankets and covers. The quilt slips into a giant-size pillowcase made from the fashionable sheeting that protects it from soil and at the same time completes the made-up bed. Be sure to buy one that is 18 inches wider than your mattress for the tuck-in allowance. Always protect your quilt from dust and dirt with its cover and occasionally hang it outside for a good airing.

How to Buy Carpets

The right carpet does wonders for any decorating scheme by adding warmth and luxuriousness and filling in those bare spots you can't afford to furnish just yet. But which rug or carpet is the best choice for you? Actually, your final decision will be based on four separate elements—color, style, quality, and price.

CHOOSE COLOR FIRST

All carpet colors available today fall into one of seven basic families—blues, greens, golds, reds, grays, beiges, and browns. Within each family there are variations from light to dark in solid colors and mixtures of hue. This wide variety enables you to choose the color you like in a version that is most practical for your purposes. If you like light colors and want to use them in a heavy-traffic area, it's best to select a two-tone mixture or tweedy effect. These don't show soil as readily as solid colors and they can add interest to a decorating scheme.

TEXTURE AND PATTERN

The pile surface of a carpet can be plain or show definite texture interest. It can have a definite pattern, muted pattern, or no pattern at all. For formal rooms, the texture known as plush is particularly suitable—a plain, cut pile with a luxurious look. Sculptured or carved effects also tend toward elegance, while loops or twists have a more rugged feeling that many people like for informal settings or as a contrast to the sleek look associated with contemporary design.

Pattern is also important and must be chosen with care. A muted pattern harmonizes with a variety of decorating schemes, but some of the definitive patterns are meant to underscore particular styles—delicate, tiny flowers would suit some small-in-scale traditional furniture, for example, but be wrong with large or heavy pieces. Above all, observe the rule that only one pattern should dominate a room. Since walls and floors are both major surfaces, use pattern on one or the other but not both. Treat sculptured textures and tone-on-tone patterns as if they were solid colors. This effect of "pattern" on the floor is subtle and adds interest without dominating the room or excluding the use of pattern elsewhere. Small patterns are generally best in small rooms and large patterns in large rooms.

If you find a patterned carpet you particularly like, you may want to build a color scheme around it, picking up one or two of the dominant colors in the pattern for solid drapery and upholstery fabrics. Conversely, you may select your carpet color from one of the tones in a patterned fabric. In either case, it is usually best to have the carpet darker in tone than the walls. This gives a room better balance.

THINK ABOUT SIZE

Carpeting today is used in three forms—wall-to-wall, room-size rugs, and area rugs.

Wall-to-wall covers the floor completely and makes a room seem more spacious because of the unbroken area of color and texture, and it offers the advantage of one surface for easy cleaning. The term broadloom is often erroneously used as a synonym for wall-to-wall, but broadloom is simply a term of measurement and indicates that a rug or carpet was made wider than six feet.

Large rugs are available in prefinished standard sizes, such as 9 by 12 feet or 12 by 15 feet, or they can be cut to desired size from rolls of carpet. Room-size rugs generally leave a border of bare floor showing—about 8 to 12 inches. They offer good value because they can be turned to distribute wear evenly and moved to another location.

Area rugs range in size from 3 by 5 feet and upward and come in varied shapes—round, oval, rectangular, or free form. They define an area of a room, accenting it with color and design. Consider room proportions in selecting size to avoid the "postage stamp" look of a skimpy rug in a large area.

A popular decorating device today is the use of more than one area rug in a large room that serves two or more functions. In a combined living and dining room, for example, a rectangular rug might be used for the main seating area and a companion rug in oval, round, or octagonal shape for the adjacent dining area.

SELECT QUALITY

When you choose a beautiful carpet, you want it to last, so give some consideration to how your carpet will look in use and how long the surface pile and the backing material will stand up.

Actually, you've already considered one aspect of performance in choosing color and texture. Medium colors, color mixtures, and patterns are best at disguising signs of use between cleaning, and loops or twists don't show footprints as readily as plain, cut piles. To select the right quality for durability, ask these questions:

1. How long do you expect your rug or carpet to last? Is this an investment for a permanent home or a temporary expedient?

2. How much use will your carpet get? Do you entertain a lot?

3. Where will your rug or carpet be used? In a daily-traffic area, a guest room, or must it meet the test of a one-room apartment?

Consider your needs, then measure traffic against quality, using the top grades in heavy-traffic areas like the living room, hallways, and stairs. Middle grades are suitable for a dining room, study, or bedroom. Economy grades will do for guest rooms or for any room in an apartment you expect to vacate soon. If you are buying wall-to-wall carpet, choose from the middle range up, since this is a permanent installation.

How can you tell whether a rug is of good quality or not? "The deeper, the denser, the better" is a good phrase to keep in mind when you shop. The more fiber packed into a carpet, the better its chances for longevity, because the yarns support each other and resist bending and abrasion.

CONSTRUCTION

Almost all carpet sold in this country is tufted, woven, or knitted. In weaving and knitting, surface yarn and backing are interlocked simultaneously, whereas in tufting, surface yarns are attached to a prewoven backing. One type is not necessarily better than another—there are different grades of quality in each.

The backing holds the carpet together and prevents stretching, shrinking, and buckling. On all tufted and knitted carpets, and many woven carpets, the backing is coated with latex for security of surface yarns. Most good quality tufted carpets have an extra layer of backing for greater strength.

DECIDE ON A FIBER

Shopping for carpeting is a little easier when you are prepared in advance for the wide range of fibers now on the market.

The surface pile of carpets and rugs today can be made from any number of natural or man-made fibers. The natural fibers are wool and cotton, and those made by man are nylon, acrylic and modacrylic, rayon, and polypropylene. Any of these can give good performance, but all do have their own characteristics.

Wool is the classic fiber, with a balance of desirable characteristics. Resiliency, abrasion-resistance, adaptability to styling, warmth and comfort to the touch, and soil-resistance are wool's traditional qualities, which are at their best in medium-to-higher-price carpets. All carpet wool used by American manufacturers is imported from countries with rugged climates, since domestic wool is too soft and fine for sturdy carpet use.

Other fibers may rate higher on one or more of the desirable characteristics for carpet use. Nylon, for example, is noted for abrasion-resistance and offers outstanding value in medium-price carpets for heavy-traffic use. There are two types of nylon—staple and continuous filament. The latter was designed to eliminate the tendency to fuzzing and pilling. Nylon is a smooth fiber that resists rapid water absorption, which means water-soluble stains are easily removed.

Acrylics and their close cousins, modacrylics, are the synthetics that most closely resemble wool—in abrasion-resistance, resiliency, softness, and warmth. Like nylon, they resist rapid water absorption.

Rayons are noted for economy and adaptability to styling. They tend to crush, although less so if the pile is very dense, but they can be used to advantage in low-traffic areas.

Polypropylene is extremely moisture-resistant and high in abrasion-resistance.

FIBER BLENDS

Two fibers are often combined in a blend in order to give the advantages of both. The higher the percentage of a particular fiber, the more a carpet will be like that fiber. For example, when wool is reinforced by nylon in a blend of 70 percent wool and 30 percent nylon, the carpet will look and feel most like wool. At least 20 percent of a fiber must be used before its characteristics are effective.

Exact fiber content must be stated on a carpet label or on the store's invoice, so check and be sure of what you are buying.

THE IMPORTANCE OF PADDING

Padding adds comfort, quiet, and insulation to a carpet. It acts as a shock absorber and, therefore, extends the life of rugs or wall-to-wall carpet.

Two types of padding are available—the felted type, generally made of hair, and rubber types. Felted hair is somewhat firmer than the bouncy rubber pads, and choosing between the two is a matter of personal preference. Felted pads are judged by weights based on ounces per square yard. Normally, a 40-ounce pad is good for home use. Rubber cushionings come in various thicknesses ranging from ⅛ inch to ½ inch (¼ inch or ⅜ inch is sufficient for household traffic).

HOW MUCH SHOULD YOU SPEND?

Value in a rug or carpet depends on price in relation to performance. A low price for poor quality is no bargain. If you pay a little more, you get a lot more. The cost of a carpet reflects many factors, including construction, fiber content, and appearance.

A certain amount of cost must go into the backing and construction of any carpet or rug. For every dollar over this amount, you add ounces of surface pile weight, which make a big difference in wear. That's why two carpets can be made of the same fiber and, at first glance, have a similar appearance, but different price tags. The more expensive one offers a better backing, superior construction, and more fiber per square inch.

Unusual styling may add to the cost of a carpet, but today a wide range of style is available in all price ranges. If you want a very unusual color, many carpets can be custom-dyed to your specifications, usually at an extra cost of a dollar or two per square yard.

To determine the real cost, consider the years of expected wear in comparison to price. If one carpet costs $5 per square yard and can be expected to wear about two years, you are actually paying $2.50 per yard per year. Another carpet costing $10 per square yard, but lasting ten years, will cost only $1 per yard per year. The more expensive carpet is actually the better bargain.

SHOPPING TIPS

To sum up, buying a rug or carpet is an important purchase and you would do well to follow this shopping guide:

1. Consider the area in which you plan to use a carpet or rug, make preliminary measurements, then let the salesman help you in making the choice best suited to your needs and preferences.

2. Beware of fantastic "bargains" and don't buy a carpet that isn't properly labeled. Good manufacturers and stores will stand behind products, so look for brand names.

3. Take a look at the many new colors and textures available— don't limit your thinking. Pick a color family you like and look for variations within that range.

4. Take a carpet sample home and see it in your room.

5. Once you've found the color and texture you like, consider performance in relation to your own needs. Don't hesitate to feel and examine closely the carpets you are considering. Look for density—the closeness of construction, the heftiness of surface pile.

6. Don't choose a carpet on the basis of fiber content alone, but do identify the fiber content and consider it in relation to quality of construction and the appearance that pleases you.

7. Don't skimp on quality for carpets and rugs that will see constant duty underfoot. Remember that poor quality carpeting is not a wise investment, but carpets and rugs of good quality will pay off in years of service and comfort.

Caring for Your Carpets

A good carpet will serve you longer and look better if you give it good care. Dirt particles are abrasives, and, if you allow them to pile up, footsteps will grind them into your carpet and create damaging friction. Soil also creates a film that dulls and changes the color you chose so carefully.

DAILY CARE

A vacuum cleaner is essential for proper carpet care. The cleaner that does the best job combines a strong suction with a revolving agitator brush or bar. Upright cleaners are usually of this type. Some canister and tank types have attachments that contain the necessary agitator, but others offer only suction. The straight suction type will remove surface dust, but not imbedded dirt.

Carpet sweepers take up lint, crumbs, and other litter from the surface and remove some dust, but they do not reach imbedded soil and are helpful only for light cleaning. Brooms sweep dust from the carpet, but toss it into the air to fall back or settle on furniture. A light brooming is helpful in brushing up a matted area, but keep it light and never use a metal broom or very stiff brush.

HOME-CLEANING METHODS

There are two ways to clean your rug—the dry method, using an absorbent powder cleaner; and the wet method, using a water-and-detergent solution. Powders are recommended for large areas, while the wet method is best suited to small areas.

Powder-type cleaners are solvent-saturated sawdust or other inert powdered material. Generally, the method calls for thorough vacuuming, then sprinkling the powder liberally over the area, brushing it into the carpet, and vacuuming it out again. Although this procedure will not clean the carpet as thoroughly as the wet method, it has the advantage of less texture distortion, better removal of greasy soil, and less drying time.

Wet cleaning is suitable for all types of carpet. Certain precautions must be taken, however, most important of which is to avoid the use of soap, ammonia, washing soda, or any strong household cleaning agents intended for hard surfaces. Use instead one of the light neutral detergents that are often sold as special-purpose cleaners for home laundering. A small amount (two heaping tablespoons to a gallon of water) provides a safe solution.

Apply this mixture sparingly with a sponge or cloth and with a gentle motion to avoid distortion of pile. Wet only the face of the carpet, not the backing. Dry as quickly as possible, using a fan if one is available.

In home-cleaning, it is not possible to rinse the carpet as would be done in a plant, and the repeated use of the detergent/water solution may leave a residue that will cause resoiling to occur more rapidly. Frequent cleanings of this type are not recommended.

PROFESSIONAL CLEANING

About once a year, you should treat your carpets to a professional cleaning that thoroughly removes all the imbedded soil you may have missed. If you have wall-to-wall carpeting, you can have someone come to your home for "on-location" cleaning, which is economical because the floor covering does not have to be taken up and then relaid.

Curtain, Drapery, and Upholstery Fabrics

Shopping was simpler, if less exciting, in the days before test tubes began bubbling in the laboratories of fabric manufacturers. Today, there are dozens of different synthetics, some claiming to work miracles right in your living room.

If you don't look for miracles, but merely good performance and a minimum of care, you'll find many synthetic fabrics that will amaze you for their ability to combine high fashion and durability with low price. In addition, the old standbys—cotton and linen— are still popular and better than ever before, thanks to modern finishing techniques and special processes that have endowed nature's own fibers with such man-made characteristics as wrinkle-resistance or spot-resistance.

WHAT TO LOOK FOR

Curtain and drapery fabrics should be reasonably resistant to sunlight, which can cause fading and deterioration. Upholstery should be firmly woven, strong enough to hold up under tension, and to resist abrasion, or the wear and tear of continual contact. All fabrics should hold their shape without excessive shrinkage or stretching, either from use or from laundering or dry cleaning.

Fiber content and the method of weaving determine these important factors of performance. Since no single fiber is perfect, fabrics are often woven in blends—either a combination of synthetics, or natural and synthetic fibers. The Federal government requires that the fiber content of every fabric be indicated on a tag, whether the fabric is sold by the yard or bought in the form of upholstery or ready-made curtains. Percentages must be shown also, and they are your best indication of how a fabric will perform.

Treating your fabrics to a stain-repelling finish is an excellent idea. "Scotchgard," "Zepel," etc., must be applied at the time of manufacture, so be sure to inquire about having this done when you are buying upholstered furniture.

New Homemaker's Checklists

Use the checklists on the following pages to formulate a purchase plan for items you want in your first home. Once you know exactly what you need to set up housekeeping, it is much easier to work out a sensible budget.

LIVING ROOM	BUY NOW	PROBABLE COST	BUY LATER	PROBABLE COST
Sofa				
Chairs				
End tables				
Cocktail table				
Nest of tables				
Desk				
Desk chair				
Hi-fi cabinets				
Cabinets				
Bookshelves				
Rug or carpet				
Window coverings				
Slipcovers				
Lamps				
Accessories:				
TOTAL COST:				

DINING AREA	BUY NOW	PROBABLE COST	BUY LATER	PROBABLE COST
Table				
Chairs				
Buffet				
Hutch				
Serving cart				
Rug or carpet				
Window coverings				
Light fixtures				
Accessories:				
TOTAL COST:				

BEDROOM	BUY NOW	PROBABLE COST	BUY LATER	PROBABLE COST
Mattress set				
Headboard				
Bed frame				
Dresser				
Chest				
Blanket chest				
Night tables				
Chair				
Lamps				
Desk				
Vanity				
Mirror				
Bedspread				
Rug or carpet				
Window coverings				
Accessories:				
TOTAL COST:				

FLATWARE	MFR.	QTY.	RECD.
PATTERN			
PLACE SETTINGS			
Place knives			
Place forks			
Place or soup spoons			
Salad forks			
Teaspoons			
Butter spreaders			
OTHER USEFUL PLACE PIECES			
Cocktail or oyster forks			
Additional teaspoons			
Iced beverage spoons			
Coffee or cocktail spoons			
Steak knives			
IMPORTANT SERVING PIECES			
Table serving spoons			
Gravy ladle			
Sugar spoon			
Butter serving knife			
Tomato or flat server			
Jelly server			
Pie or cake server			
Salad set			
Cold meat or buffet fork			
Carving set			
Cream or sauce ladle			
INFORMAL FLATWARE PATTERN			
Service for			

GLASSWARE	MFR.	QTY.	RECD.
PATTERN			
Water goblet			
Champagne			
Wine			
Sherbet			
Iced tea			
Tumbler			
Juice			
Sherry			
Liqueur			
Brandy			
Beer			
Pitchers			
Dessert plates			
Ashtrays and urns			
Punch bowl set			
Cruets			
Relish dish			
Decanters			
BAR ACCESSORIES			
Old-Fashioned			
Highball			
Martini			
Whiskey sour			
Measuring glass			
Cocktail shaker			
Ice bucket			

HOLLOWARE	MFR.	PTRN.	RECD.
Well-and-tree platter			
Vegetable dishes			
Serving trays			
Buffet dishes			
Gravy boat			
Bread tray			
Bowls			
Salts and peppers			
Pitchers			
Tea service			
Coffee service			
Sugar and creamer			
Candlesticks			
Candelabra			
Ashtrays			

DINNERWARE	MFR.	QTY.	RECD.
PATTERN			
PLACE SETTINGS			
Cereal saucers			
Soup plates			
Meat platter			
Salad bowl			
Vegetable dishes			
Cream soups			
Fruit bowls			
Demitasse cups			
Gravy boat			
Chop plate			
Soup tureen			
Coffeepot			
Teapot			
Sugar and creamer			
Set of informal			

LINENS	MFR.	CLR.	QTY.	RECD.
TABLE LINENS				
Dinner cloth and napkins				
Extra dinner napkins				
Luncheon cloth and napkins				
Tea cloth and napkins				
Formal mat sets				
Informal mat sets				
Bridge table cloth				
Cocktail napkins				
BATH LINENS				
Bath towels				
Hand towels				
Washcloths				
Fingertip towels				
Guest towels				
Bath mat				
Rug and lid set				
Shower curtain				
BED LINENS				
Flat sheets				
Fitted sheets				
Pillowcases				
Pillows				
Winter-weight blankets				
Summer-weight blankets				
Comforters				
Automatic blankets				
Mattress pads				
Blanket covers				
Pillow covers				
Bedspreads				
Dust ruffles				
KITCHEN LINENS				
Dish towels				
Glass towels				
Dish cloths				
Pot holders				
Appliance covers				
Aprons				

KITCHEN	SIZE	MFR.	RECD.
COLOR SCHEME			
Coffee maker			
Tea kettle			
Covered saucepans (1, 2, and 4 qt.)			
Double boiler			
Small and large skillets			
Egg poacher			
Dutch oven			
Casseroles			
Pressure cooker			
Roasting pan and rack			
Cake pans			
Muffin tins			
Cookie sheets			
Pie pans			
Colander			
Molds			
Mixing bowls			
Canisters			
Measuring spoons, cups			
Wooden spoon			
Utensil set (spoon, fork, ladle, etc.)			
Carving knife set			
Paring knives			
Bread knife			
Salt and pepper set			
Can opener			
Food chopper			
Cutting board			
Funnel			
Egg beater			
Meat thermometer			
Timer			
Baster			
Pastry brush			
Grater			
Juicer			
Strainer			
Vegetable peeler			
Corkscrew			